GALATIANS

ABINGDON NEW TESTAMENT COMMENTARIES

GALATIANS

SAM K. WILLIAMS

Abingdon Press
Nashville

ABINGDON NEW TESTAMENT COMMENTARIES:
GALATIANS

Copyright © 1997 by Abingdon Press

This book is printed on recycled, acid-free, elemental-chlorine–free paper.

Library of Congress Cataloging-in-Publication Data

Williams, Sam K.
   Galatians / Sam K. Williams.
      p. cm. — (Abingdon New Testament commentaries)
   Includes bibliographical references and index.
   ISBN 0-687-05707-8 (pbk. : alk. paper)
   1. Bible. N.T. Galatians—Commentaries. I. Title. II. Series.
BS2685.3.W534   1997
227'.407—dc21   97-13815
                                                CIP

Scripture quotations noted as AT are the author's translation.

97 98 99 00 01 02 03 04 05 06—10 9 8 7 6 5 4 3 2 1

MANUFACTUED IN THE UNITED STATES OF AMERICA

To my mother
Mary Louise Rives Williams
with affection and appreciation

and to the memory of my father
Samuel Cicero Williams
(1911–1950)

CONTENTS

FOREWORD

The *Abingdon New Testament Commentaries* series provides compact, critical commentaries on the writings of the New Testament. These commentaries are written with special attention to the needs and interests of theological students, but they will also be useful for students in upper-level college or university settings, as well as for pastors and other church leaders. In addition to providing basic information about the New Testament texts and insights into their meanings, these commentaries are intended to exemplify the tasks and procedures of careful, critical biblical exegesis.

The authors who have contributed to this series come from a wide range of ecclesiastical affiliations and confessional stances. All are seasoned, respected scholars and experienced classroom teachers. They take full account of the most important current scholarship and secondary literature, but do not attempt to summarize that literature or to engage in technical academic debate. Their fundamental concern is to analyze the literary, socio-historical, theological, and ethical dimensions of the biblical texts themselves. Although all of the commentaries in this series have been written on the basis of the Greek texts, the authors do not presuppose any knowledge of the biblical languages on the part of the reader. When some awareness of a grammatical, syntactical, or philological issue is necessary for an adequate understanding of a particular text, they explain the matter clearly and concisely.

The introduction of each volume ordinarily includes subdivisions dealing with the *key issues* addressed and/or raised by the New Testament writing under consideration; its *literary genre, structure, and character;* its *occasion and situational context,* including its wider social, historical, and religious contexts; and its *theological and ethical significance* within these several contexts.

In each volume, the *commentary* is organized according to literary units rather than verse by verse. Generally, each of these units is the subject of three types of analysis. First, the *literary analysis* attends to the unit's genre, most important stylistic features, and overall structure. Second, the *exegetical analysis* considers the aim and leading ideas of the unit, deals with any especially important textual variants, and discusses the meanings of important words, phrases, and images. It also takes note of the particular historical and social situations of the writer and original readers, and of the wider cultural and religious contexts of the book as a whole. Finally, the *theological and ethical analysis* discusses the theological and ethical matters with which the unit deals or to which it points, focusing on the theological and ethical significance of the text within its original setting.

Each volume also includes a *select bibliography,* thereby providing guidance to other major commentaries and important scholarly works, and a brief *subject index.* The New Revised Standard Version of the Bible is the principal translation of reference for the series, but the authors draw on all of the major modern English versions, and when necessary provide their own original translations of difficult terms or phrases.

The fundamental aim of this series will have been attained if readers are assisted, not only to understand more about the origins, character, and meaning of the New Testament writings, but also to enter into their own informed and critical engagement with the texts themselves.

Victor Paul Furnish
General Editor

PREFACE

I am grateful to Colorado College for a Research and Development Block and a semester-long sabbatical that enabled me to complete this commentary on Paul's Letter to the Christians of Galatia.

As the deadline for completion of my manuscript moved relentlessly closer, my colleagues Joseph Pickle and Douglas Fox—each for a year—spared me the duties of chairing the Colorado College Department of Religion. Students in my 1995 Galatians Seminar launched me into a productive summer of writing. For more than a year, members of the Fellowship Class of First Baptist Church, Colorado Springs, listened and responded, during the Sunday school hour, to an earlier draft of the commentary. Rory Stadler and Ed Winograd provided indispensable assistance with a word processing program that sometimes stymied my own inexpert efforts. No less crucial was the encouragement of Pheme Perkins and Victor Paul Furnish, whose suggestions helped me shorten the manuscript so that it conformed more closely to the aims of the *Abingdon New Testament Commentaries* series. To all these friends and coworkers, my sincere appreciation and heartiest thanks!

Two prefatory words about conventions I have used in this commentary are in order. First, although "Christian" and "Christianity" appear here, I have often preferred to use such expressions as "Jesus-people," "Jesus-communities," and "Jesus-movement" in order to remind readers that, when used to name a first-century phenomenon and persons, "Christianity" and "Christians" are anachronistic—these words having not yet been coined.

Second, by "symbolic world" I mean that constellation of values, meanings, and convictions about the nature of things that determine human perception, decision, and action. Socially shared rather than private and idiosyncratic, a symbolic world manifests itself most clearly in those beliefs and values that members of a community or society take for granted, those ideas and practices that need no defense or justification because everyone "just knows" that they are right or true. (For a more technical definition and more detailed analysis of "symbolic world," see Berger and Luckmann 1966, and Berger 1967.)

Finally, a note on inclusive langage. Assuming that Paul cannot be ignoring the female members of the Galatian congregations, the NRSV consistently translates *adelphoi* as "brothers and sisters" (see Gal 1:11). Especially in light of the women named in Romans 16, the translators are likely right in thinking that Paul is not deliberately excluding the women among his hearers. Nevertheless, Paul's language in Galatians does clearly reflect the patriarchal assumptions that permeated his culture. Allowing Paul to remain a man of his own time, in this commentary I have refrained from modernizing his language.

Sam K. Williams

LIST OF ABBREVIATIONS

1QH	*Thanksgiving Hymns* (Qumran Cave 1)
1QS	*Rule of the Community* (Qumran Cave 1)
1QpHab	*Pesher on Habakkuk* (Qumran Cave 1)
ABD	D. N. Freedman (ed.), *Anchor Bible Dictionary*
Abr.	Philo, *On the Life of Abraham*
AT	Author's translation
Ant.	Josephus, *The Antiquities of the Jews*
Apoc. Abr.	*Apocalypse of Abraham*
Bib. Ant.	Pseudo-Philo, *Biblical Antiquities*
BNTC	Black's New Testament Commentaries
CBQ	*Catholic Biblical Quarterly*
FFNT	Foundations and Facets: New Testament
HR	*History of Religions*
HTR	*Harvard Theological Review*
ICC	International Critical Commentary
IDB	G. A. Buttrick (ed.), *Interpreter's Dictionary of the Bible*
JBL	*Journal of Biblical Literature*
JSNT	*Journal for the Study of the New Testament*
JSNTSup	Journal for the Study of the New Testament —Supplement Series
JSOT	*Journal for the Study of the Old Testament*
JTS	*Journal of Theological Studies*
Jub.	*Jubilees*
LXX	Septuagint
MeyerC	H. A. W. Meyer, Critical and Exegetical Commentary on the New Testament

MeyerK	H. A. W. Meyer, Kritisch-exegetischer Kommentar über das Neue Testament
MNTC	Moffatt NT Commentary
NICNT	New International Commentary on the New Testament
NIGTC	The New International Greek Testament Commentary
NovT	*Novum Testamentum*
NRSV	New Revised Standard Version
NTS	*New Testament Studies*
RelS	*Religious Studies*
RelSRev	*Religious Studies Review*
SBLDS	SBL Dissertation Series
SBLSP	SBL Seminar Papers
SP	Sacra Pagina
Spec. Leg.	Philo, *On the Special Laws*
SJT	*Scottish Journal of Theology*
Virt.	Philo, *On Virtue*
WBC	Word Biblical Commentary

INTRODUCTION

APPROACHING GALATIANS

Why do people read Galatians today? They might have several reasons. First, whatever else it is, Galatians is also an important cultural artifact. Written in the first generation of the Jesus-movement, it contributes significantly to our understanding of the religious and cultural life of the Mediterranean world at the beginning of the common era. More specifically, Galatians is an important witness to a crucial moment in the development of Christianity from a Jewish sectarian movement to a Gentile religion.

Second, Galatians is much more than a historical source. It is a historic document as well. Its authority assured by its being included in the Christian canon of Scripture, Galatians has exercised enormous influence on the development of Christian institutions and theology, from Marcion in the second century to advocates of liberation theology in the twentieth (see Longenecker 1990, xliii-lvii). Most notable, perhaps, Martin Luther's fondness for Galatians made it one of the pillars of the Protestant Reformation.

A third reason to read Galatians is this: the letter affords a fascinating glimpse of how Paul negotiated a reconciliation between his Jewish heritage and the new understanding of self and God and world traceable to the conversion that transformed him into an apostle of Christ. This glimpse raises intriguing questions about the authority of scripture over against the authority of personal experience.

For Christians, these reasons for reading Galatians are, at best, secondary, for the Bible is the "word of God" and Galatians is a centrally important part of that word. Because of its rhetorical power and its important theological emphases—grace, faith, justification, freedom and life in Christ, the fruit of the Spirit, new creation—this Pauline letter, Christians believe, can be a medium through which God still addresses humankind.

In this commentary I want to try to "overhear" Galatians as though I were present in one of the Galatian house-church assemblies as the letter was being read. This goal, I hasten to add, is impossible to attain. I cannot hear Paul's letter as his first auditors did. Too much separates us. We are strangers to one another. My symbolic world is almost unimaginably different from theirs. Mine, for example, is permeated at every point by the presuppositions and consequences of the natural sciences; theirs was pre-scientific, their common question not *what* but *who* caused this—and why? My social and economic world is post-industrial and technological; theirs, pre-industrial and agrarian, glassblowing and the vertical loom exemplary of their latest technological advances (Koester 1982, 1:77, 79). In my society the goal of upward social mobility informs the life expectations of many; in theirs, life's opportunities depended heavily, for most people, on the class and family they were born into. In my society individualism reigns supreme; in theirs, *communal* values provided a steady antidote to private ambition and selfishness. The self-understanding of most twentieth-century Westerners draws heavily from the introspective conscience, which, though explored by Augustine, was virtually unknown to Paul and his contemporaries (Stendahl 1963).

In a world in which most persons were subject to powers, human and divine, over which they had only minimal control, talk of divine grace and justification probably sounded much different than to readers of the Bible two thousand years later. In Western democracies today, even with all the frustrations that people bear, the powers of surgery, technology, and social planning enable most of us to assume a degree of control over our lives—personal and social— utterly foreign to the first century. It is, accordingly, not "second nature" for most moderns to think of their ultimate well-being in terms of "grace" or "justification," the gifts of Another. Even many religious people have to work at this way of thinking, imposing, as it were, an alien scheme upon their more natural habits of thought. In spite of our best efforts, then, are any of us *able* really to hear

Paul today? I, for one, am not willing to answer that question with a quick and confident "Of course."

The goal of overhearing is nevertheless significant, at least regarding method and approach. Constrained by the effort to overhear, I deliberately try to bracket out nineteen hundred years of Christian theologizing. I do not appeal to interpretive aids that the Galatians would not have had available to them. In particular, I do not appeal to arguments or word usage specific to other New Testament writings, even other Pauline letters. Nor do I attempt to fit Galatians into some preconceived notion of "Pauline theology."

PAUL AND THE GALATIANS

The text of Galatians leaves no doubt that Paul is trying to *affect* the recipients of the letter. This attempt would be pointless if he was not able to presume that what he thinks about the issue at hand *matters* to them. He can assume that they care what he thinks because, somehow, his views have a bearing on their well-being. The connection between their well-being and his views is to be sought in the history of their relationship. Who were the parties to this relationship? Who was Paul? Who were the Galatians?

The Apostle

Like all of us, Paul moved in several "worlds." He moved literally in the natural world of the Mediterranean basin, whose climate, weather, and topography affected his travels. Apart from the physical reality of geographical distance, there would be no Letter to the Galatians. More significantly, though, Paul moved in several worlds created by people, the various worlds of human culture—from kinship arrangements and political organization to religious practices and convictions about the nature of things.

Emperor and the mechanisms of empire (organization, administration, taxation, the military suppression of conquered peoples) dominated Paul's political world. Roman roads facilitated his travels, as did the freedom from war and internal danger that marked the "peace of Rome" that had begun with Augustus. At the same time, Rome's policies contributed to a widespread sense of alienation and fatalism on the part of her subjects. Class and gender hierarchy shaped Paul's stratified social world, and the dynamics of hierarchy played themselves out in the family and in the institution of slavery. Although manumission was not uncommon, slavery was such a prominent feature of the first-century social world that one New Testament scholar can claim that Paul defines the human condition itself as enslavement to one master or another (Petersen 1985, 245).

The religious world in which Paul moved touted magic and astrology, miracle and spiritual ecstasy as means of deliverance from powers—human and cosmic—that constrained human life. Various new eastern cults (e.g., those of Isis, Mithras, and Cybele) competed with more established religious traditions for the hearts and minds of people who longed for a sense of worth and meaning, revelation, and personal transformation. Popular philosophies like Stoicism, Epicureanism, and Cynicism offered their diagnostic and therapeutic insights (Johnson 1986, 23-39; see also Malina 1981 on the first-century Mediterranean world).

Although the political, cultural, social, and religious ideas and institutions of his time contributed significantly, Paul's symbolic world was, above all, the system of beliefs and customs he was born into as a Jew. Central to the Judaisms that shaped his life, whether Palestinian Pharisaic or Hellenistic Diaspora, were the worship of the one God and the conviction that God had elected Israel from all the peoples of the earth for a unique relationship with the deity and for the special task of being a holy people in a corrupt world. How Israel was to live and worship, God had revealed in Torah, the laws and narratives that were, in effect, the "constitution" of God's people. Covenant, Temple, and Torah thus structured the lives of all faithful Jews and provided them a distinct identity. Paul describes himself as a Jew of enviable religious pedigree who was particularly zealous for the ancestral traditions and "blameless" with respect to Torah. It was, indeed, his religious zeal that incited him to persecute the young Jesus-movement (Gal 1:13-14; Phil 3:4-6).

But something happened to Paul that transformed him from a persecutor of the church to a passionate proclaimer of the gospel and a tireless shepherd of Jesus-congregations. He writes very little about that experience, but three passages permit us to see that he understands it as a revelation from the realm of the divine, a revelation of God's crucified and resurrected Messiah (1 Cor 9:1; 15:3-8; Gal 1:15-16). This experience effected a fundamental reconfiguration of Paul's symbolic world, and apart from it his subsequent behavior and belief are inexplicable. But at the center of Paul's convictions and behavior, as both persecutor and apostle, loomed the immense reality of God, the creator, savior, and judge whose purpose for the creation was being fulfilled. In God's plan for the final days the apostle knew he had been called to play an indispensable role.

The Galatians

That the recipients of this letter were Gentiles (at least predominantly so) is clear from 4:8-9; 5:2-3; 6:12-13. The letter seems to presuppose, however, that they were quite familiar with Jewish Scripture and principles of biblical interpretation. This familiarity was likely due, in part, to Paul's initial preaching among them and to the teachings of certain outside agitators. New Testament scholars have long been convinced, though, that many of Paul's Gentile converts had already been attracted to Judaism prior to becoming Jesus-people (on the "God-fearers," see Fredriksen 1991, 541-43). Their attraction to the synagogue and their familiarity with Judaism would nicely explain why the Galatians had welcomed Paul as a messenger *(angelos)* of God, even as Messiah Jesus (4:14).

The recipients of the letter were also, of course, Galatians. But who were *they*? The reply "inhabitants of Galatia" does not take us very far because "Galatia" can name either an ethnic territory or a Roman province. The territory Galatia takes its name from Celtic tribes from central Europe who, in the third century BCE, invaded and settled in western and central Asia Minor. In the last third of that century, the king of Pergamum confined them to an area bounded by Bithynia and Paphlagonia, Pontus and Cappadocia, Lycaonia and Phrygia. In 189 BCE, Galatia, like the rest of Asia Minor, came under Roman rule, and in 64 BCE Pompey designated Galatia a client kingdom of Rome. When the last client king of

Galatia was killed in 25 BCE, this territory was reorganized as a Roman province, and in subsequent years this province was expanded to include parts of Paphlagonia, Pontus, Pamphylia, Lycaonia, and Phrygia (Ramsay 1899).

The absence of decisive evidence has prevented scholarly consensus about the location of "the churches of Galatia" (1:2). According to the "North Galatian" or "territory" theory, they were located in the ethnic territory of Galatia, whose major cities were Pessinus, Ancyra, and Tavium. According to the "South Galatian" or "province" theory, they were in the much larger Roman province of Galatia, which included the cities of Derbe, Lystra, and Iconium. For the following reasons the province theory is preferred here.

Paul does not say what cities in Syria and Cilicia (Gal 1:21) he was active in, but after his Damascus period (1:17) all the cities he names as the locales of his ministry are on or very near the sea: Antioch, Ephesus, Troas, Philippi, Thessalonica, Athens, Corinth. This fact creates a presumption in favor of the Galatian churches being located in southern Asia Minor rather than farther north. So does the fact that in the mid-first century, travel was easier in southern Asia Minor than in the north-central region. Whereas the main Roman highway *(via Sebaste)* linking most of the major cities of the south was built before 6 BCE, Roman roads in the northern part of the Galatian provinice were constructed only in the 70s and 80s CE (Mitchell 1992).

Paul calls the other regions where his churches are located "Asia," "Macedonia," and "Achaia" (e.g., Rom 16:5, 1 Cor 16:19, 2 Cor 1:8. Rom 15:26; 1 Cor 16:5; 2 Cor 1:16, 8:1, 11:9. 1 Cor 16:15; 2 Cor 1:1; 9:2; 1 Thess 1:7). These are all names of Roman provinces. One might argue, of course, that in each of these cases (unlike the case of Galatia) no commonly used term was available to name an ethnic territory as distinct from an administrative province. Nevertheless, the very fact that Paul can speak of "Asia" when he seems to have in mind Ephesus and perhaps its environs (cf. 1 Cor 16:19 with 16:8, and 2 Cor 1:8 with 1 Cor 15:32*a*) encourages the view that he thinks, geographically, in terms of the administrative units of the Roman Empire.

A distinct implication of Paul's wording at Gal 4:13 is that the region in which the Galatian churches were located had not been

Current Check-Outs Summary for GARCIA, L
15 15:46:47 CST 2012

BARCODE: 3.45004188737
TITLE: Martin Luther : the best
DUE DATE: Jan 30 2012
DESENSITIZED: true

BARCODE: 32345025/1913
TITLE: Galatians / Sam K. Williams.
DUE DATE: Jan 30 2012
DESENSITIZED: true

on his planned mission itinerary at the time he first preached the gospel there: it was *because of* a "physical infirmity" that he had proclaimed the gospel to the Galatians. It would appear that he had been on his way to somewhere *else,* changing his plans because of the affliction he mentions, but making good use of his unexpected situation by evangelizing until he was able to resume the journey planned. It is much easier to imagine Paul passing through the southern region of the Galatian *province* than through ethnic Galatia en route to somewhere else on a planned mission. Similarly, whether we think of the Galatian agitators as Jewish-Christian missionaries with their own Law-observant mission or as interlopers who dogged Paul and tried to set his converts straight, it is easier to envision them making their way into southern Asia Minor than into the interior regions of ethnic Galatia.

As noted earlier, many scholars think that Paul's Galatian converts had been associated with the synagogue and familiar with Jewish Scripture prior to becoming Jesus-people. Familiarity with Judaism would, of course, be more likely in a region with a relatively sizable Jewish population, and in the first century the Jewish presence was more substantial in southern Asia Minor than farther north. Prior to Roman domination of the area, the Seleucid kings had favored Jews as settlers in their Asian colonies, almost all of which lay on the southern side of the Anatolian plateau and chiefly along the east-west lines of communication (Ramsay 1899, 88).

To hold that "the churches of Galatia" were in the southern part of the Roman province is not to conclude that they were located in Antioch, Iconium, Lystra, and Derbe. If Paul's preaching ministry in Galatia was unplanned, as 4:13 strongly implies, would he have founded congregations so widely separated from one another as were these four cities? In light of 4:13, even the assumption that the Galatian congregations were located in urban centers is not certain. The Christians to whom Paul writes might have lived in all, some, one, or none of these cities and their environs. The fact is that we cannot know. With more assurance one can say that they were at least predominantly Gentiles (4:8), familiar with, and affected by, Judaism, who had embraced the Pauline gospel with some enthusiasm (4:14-15).

Paul's Relationship with the Galatians

The writing and receiving of Galatians are but two moments in a narrative continuum whose starting point was Paul's initial preaching to the Galatians and whose next chapter will be the decisions, and resulting behavior, Paul hopes his letter will effect. This narrative of the Paul/Galatians relationship is set in the longer story of God's dealings with humankind—a story that stretches from God's promise to Abraham to God's final judgment and includes, as its most decisive moment, the death and resurrection of Jesus.

As already noted, Gal 4:13 gives the unavoidable impression that Paul's initial contact with the Galatians had not been planned. He writes: "You know that it was because of a physical infirmity that I first announced the gospel to you." Apparently, then, the persons to whom he now writes lived in cities or villages that had not been on the apostle's missionary itinerary. They could thus regard his infirmity as providential. In any case, they had welcomed him as if he were an angel of God, as if he were Christ Jesus (4:14)—and this in spite of an affliction that he characterizes as a "test" (or "trial") to them. Indeed, so intense were their affection and appreciation that they would have gouged out their eyes and given them to Paul (4:15). Why such intense feelings? Paul does not tell us (and he does not need to tell the Galatians), but a likely reason was their gratitude for the message of life that Paul had brought them.

What was the content of this message, Paul's missionary "good news"? In attempting to answer that question, we have two primary resources. One is those passages in Galatians and other letters in which Paul repeats or refers to something he had said earlier to the recipients. The second is those key terms and ideas in Galatians that Paul appears to assume the Galatians are already familiar with.

From Gal 3:1 and 1 Cor 1:21-23; 2:1-2 we learn that Paul had preached the crucified Messiah Jesus. If we can judge from 1 Cor 15:1-5, "the good news that I proclaimed to you" featured Jesus' resurrection as well as his atoning death. Jesus' *parousia* and God's final judgment were two other themes he almost certainly emphasized (see Phil 3:20; 1 Thess 5:2). Indeed, God's judgment is the prospect in light of which we are to understand the ethical admonitions that were apparently so prominent in his missionary preaching. Galatians 5:21 ("I am warning you, as I warned you before: those who do such things [the "works of the flesh" in vv. 19-21] will not inherit the kingdom of God") is by no means atypical. In 1 Thessalonians Paul recounts with obvious satisfaction what believers in Achaia and in Macedonia say about the Thessalonian Christians: "how you turned to God from idols, to serve a living and true [i.e., real] God, and to wait for his Son from heaven, whom he raised from the dead—Jesus, who rescues us from the wrath that is coming" (1 Thess 1:9-10). We can infer that the Thessalonians turned from idols in *response* to Paul's preaching and in accord with his appeal (see also Gal 4:9). The apostle apparently stressed that conversion to the one true God must find expression in lives of holiness and in conduct pleasing to God (1 Thess 2:11-12). He seems to have been particularly concerned about sexual purity (Phil 3:17-20; 1 Thess 4:1-7).

Other emphases of Paul's missionary preaching we can infer from several significant terms in Galatians that do not appear to derive from the agitators (or from the argument designed to refute them) but that Paul makes no effort to define or explain: the grace of God (or Christ) (1:6, 15; 2:9, 21), righteousness (2:21; 3:6) and being justified by God (2:16-17), the act of believing (2:16) and the "faith of [or "in"] Christ" (2:16).

Paul presumes, I have suggested, that what he thinks about the issue at hand matters to the Galatians and that it matters because his views affect their ultimate well-being. But the Galatians are not the only party whose well-being is affected by their standing fast. Paul regards himself as an emissary of the deity, commissioned by no less an authority than Godself. An emissary is honor-bound to fulfill faithfully the duties laid upon him, and Paul is at pains, literally and metaphorically, to fulfill his divine commission by establishing and nurturing congregations of Gentile believers until Jesus' *parousia*. Indeed, three quite different Pauline letters indicate that he was motivated not solely by his concern for God's other human creatures. His *own* destiny was at stake as well!

When Paul writes, "woe to me if I do not proclaim the gospel" (1 Cor 9:16), he is speaking with full seriousness. As the Hebrew word for *woe* in the prophetic writings and its Greek equivalent in early Christian literature make clear, he expects God's judgment upon himself if he fails to fulfill the obligation laid upon him. So seriously does he take his commission as apostle to the Gentiles that he is willing to "endure anything rather than put an obstacle in the way of the gospel of Christ" (1 Cor 9:12). His preaching the gospel gives him no ground for boasting (1 Cor 9:16); yet, Paul says, he disciplines himself like an athlete so that he might not be disqualified from receiving the "prize" that believers hope for at the end of the age. Philippians 2:14-16, moreover, seems to imply that he thought God's reward was contingent upon the effectiveness of his apostolic labor. To his converts in Philippi he writes: "It is by your holding fast to the word of life that I can boast on the day of Christ that I did not run in vain or labor in vain" (2:16). And he refers to the Thessalonian believers as "our hope or joy or crown of boasting before our Lord Jesus at his coming" (1 Thess 2:19-20). Later in the same letter, he explains why he had sent Timothy to find out about their faith: "I was afraid that somehow the tempter had tempted you and that our labor had been in vain" (3:5). We find the opposite of this "in vain" three verses later: "For we now live, if you continue to stand firm in the Lord" (3:8).

From the clues available in these revealing statements in 1 Corinthians, Philippians, and 1 Thessalonians, readers of Galatians can discern an unspoken reason for the intensity of Paul's response to the situation in Galatia: certain agitators were jeopardizing the spiritual well-being of Gentile believers whose membership in the people of God demonstrated his faithfulness as a God-commissioned apostle. Like the Thessalonians, the Galatians—and, indeed, *all* Paul's Gentile converts—were his hope and joy and crown of boasting. On the day of Christ he would live if they stood firm and held fast the word of life. But now they wavered, uncertain, in danger of falling out of grace and severing themselves from Christ (Gal 5:4). With their eternal destiny at stake, and his as well, it is not surprising that Paul was too troubled to be evenhanded and too angry to be polite.

OCCASION AND CONTEXT

A fourth component of the "Galatian moment" is the occasion of the letter's writing, the situation that evoked it. How did Paul know about that situation? By letter? By personal (oral) report? How full and how accurate was the information he had received? Later readers cannot know the answer to these questions, nor can we know as much as we would like about the so-called "crisis in Galatia" and the persons responsible for it. What we read in Galatians is hardly a dispassionate and impartial account of either. Paul refers to these persons as "some [people] who are confusing you" (1:7; 5:10) and "those who unsettle you" (5:12). (Thus I refer to them as "the agitators" throughout this commentary.) The two things that one can say with certainty are that the agitators are Christians (they preach a "different gospel," 1:6) who are trying to persuade the Galatian believers to be circumcised (5:2-3; 6:12-13; see 2:3-5; 5:11, 12). With only slightly less confidence one can deduce that they were Christian *Jews* (at 4:25 Paul associates them with Sinai and "the present Jerusalem") and that they came from outside the Galatian congregations (note that Paul always refers to them in the third person [1:7; 3:1; 4:17; 5:7, 12; 6:12-13] but to the Galatians in the second person [e.g., 1:6, 11; 3:1; 4:8-11, 12-20; 5:2]).

Paul's polemical charges provide an unreliable basis for characterizing the aims and motives of these Jewish-Christian missionaries. No doubt they would vigorously challenge his accusation that they want to "pervert" the gospel of Christ (1:7), nor could we expect them to share the view that they have diverted the Galatians from the goal of their spiritual journey (5:7). These charges are not subject to any sort of impartial adjudication by later readers. They are matters of opinion—Paul's opinion. On the other hand, his claims about their motives at 6:12-13 are such that certain facts known to the Galatians could render these claims either believable or incredible. If they had so little substance that they did not ring true, Paul's assertions would undermine rather than buttress his case. He charges that "it is those who want to make a good showing in the flesh that try to compel you to be circumcised—only that they may not be persecuted for the cross of Christ" (6:12); "they want you to be circumcised so that they may boast about your flesh" (6:13). How could it be that getting Gentile believers circumcised was a source of pride or glory, and how could that success protect the agitators from being "persecuted"?

Many students of Galatians find attractive the theory that the historical context of the agitators' program was a campaign undertaken by zealous Jewish nationalists to purify Israel by avoiding close relationships with Gentiles and by exterminating all impure persons. Christian Jews in Judea wished to avert the suspicion that they were in communion with lawless Gentiles, and apparently they believed that circumcision of Christian Gentiles would thwart zealot reprisals (Jewett 1970–71, 204-5). Although this theory would make good sense of the agitators' attempt to circumcise Gentile believers as an effort to avoid persecution, three weaknesses disqualify it. (1) From the late 40s until the outbreak of the war against Rome in 66, Judean nationalists were concerned with Roman political oppression. They aimed to purify the *land* that God had promised to Abraham's descendants. (2) The theory lacks credible evidence that Judean zealots targeted "impure persons" outside the land of promise. (3) The theory does not allow for the well-attested association of (non-circumcised) Gentile God-fearers with the synagogue, especially in the Diaspora.

Our earlier question therefore remains: How could their success in getting Gentile believers circumcised protect the agitators from persecution? We lack evidence that the non-circumcised state of Gentiles associated with the synagogue was ever a cause of persecution. Apparently, then, the question of the status of Gentiles in the Jesus-communities was sufficiently different from the question of God-fearers in the synagogue that some Christian Jews were insisting—under pressure, perhaps, from non-Christian Jews—that these Gentiles be circumcised. The Antioch incident (Gal 2:11-14) permits the speculation that this issue was brought to the fore by the symbolically significant association of Jewish and Gentile Jesus-people at the common meals of the community. Moreover, at Gal 5:11, as at 6:12, Paul connects being persecuted with Jesus' death: in that verse, to preach circumcision is to *deny* the scandal of the cross. One reason the preaching of the cross was scandalous to non-Christian Jews was that it offered an alternate means for Gentiles to be incorporated into the people of God: faith in place of circumcision. The threat of persecution was an understandable response by some Jews (perhaps Christian and non-Christian) to this dangerous challenge to the integrity of the ancestral religion. The agitators' pressure on Gentile believers to get circumcised was, in turn, a reasonable response to the threat of persecution. Securing the circumcision of Gentile believers would, at the least, help allay the suspicion that the Jesus-communities of the Diaspora were ignoring the key requirements of Torah.

The agitators did not wish to keep Gentiles from becoming members of the people of God, but they did insist that Gentiles comply with God's own command that circumcision be the sign of the covenant between God and God's people (Gen 17). It was probably they who raised the issue of who were the legitimate "sons of Abraham" and they who used the Abraham traditions of Genesis to substantiate their case (Martyn 1985, 318-20). Paul's Sarah/Hagar allegory is likely his response to their argument that the sons of Hagar—Gentiles—could become children of the promise only by accepting, in their flesh, the sign of God's covenant, just as Abraham had done (Martyn 1991, 184). Much of chapter 3 makes better sense if we assume the agitators insisted that Abraham's descendants, proselytes as well as those who were born Jews, must live according to the requirement of Torah. From Paul's emphasis on the divine source of his commissioning and his gospel, some students of Galatians have further concluded that the agitators challenged his apostolic credentials and thus his authority (see those cited by Lyons 1985, 81-82, n. 18).

In using the Abraham traditions for their own ends, the agitators could evidently rely on considerable rhetorical ability (3:1; 5:7-8), but their message had its own intrinsic appeal. Having abandoned the worship of pagan deities, the Galatian believers faced both cognitive readjustment and social dislocation. The agitators could offer them a clear and much-needed new social and religious identity (Barclay 1988, 58-60), and the distinctive mark of that identity was circumcision. They could also claim that the Law of

Moses provided a superior means of attaining the virtues prized in the Greco-Roman world, especially the virtue of self-mastery (Stowers 1994, 61, 71). The Galatians' experience of the Spirit (3:2-5) imparted no practical guidelines for decision and action. The Law's detailed instructions for the conduct of everyday life would have thus offered a sense of stability and security for Gentile converts who otherwise could easily feel adrift, lacking both moral criteria and rituals associated with repentance and forgiveness (Barclay 1988, 70-71 and authors cited there).

GENRE AND CHARACTER

In the hellenistic age, correspondence by letter ranged from brief notes pertaining to business or personal affairs to epistolary treatises by moralists and philosophers, poets and statesmen (Johnson 1986, 251). The "occasional" nature of Paul's letters is obvious. Most of them he wrote in response to situations in congregations he had founded that now required his attention. His letters, then, were substitutes for his personal presence. That the apostle expected them to be read aloud in the congregations when believers gathered for worship and instruction is probable *prima facie* (how else would the Christian communities, even if small, have access to his letters—especially if Paul's emissary carried only one copy or even one copy per congregation?). The directive of 1 Thess 5:27 ("that this letter be read to all") would seem to secure this likelihood.

Many letter writers in the Greco-Roman world, even those who could write, dictated their letters to a professional scribe or private secretary, an amanuensis. Certainly Paul did. In Romans his amanuensis adds his own greeting (16:22), and Paul's statement at 1 Cor 16:21 indicates that he had dictated the rest of the letter. His mention of the large letters (characters) "in my own hand" at Gal 6:11 bears the same implication. But whether Paul's amanuensis took word-by-word dictation or contributed more substantively to the composing of Galatians we have no way of knowing.

Since Galatians will be read aloud to the Galatian congregations, Paul writes (dictates) the letter to be performed as a *speech* introduced and concluded by an epistolary prescript and postscript. As a speech, the letter will therefore have been experienced by the Galatian Christians, at least initially, with the ear rather than the eye, and it will have made its first impact *as it unfolded,* for a speech is linear and cumulative; and hearers, unlike later readers, cannot leisurely contemplate, analyze, cross-check, and compare later statements with earlier ones (see Kennedy 1984, 5-6).

In recent years Pauline scholars have increasingly acknowledged the importance of rhetoric in the ancient world and thus the need to give attention to the rhetorical features of early Christian writings. Rhetoric was a central academic discipline taught throughout the Roman Empire. Aristotle, Cicero, and Quintilian were among the authors who wrote treatises on rhetoric. Numerous handbooks described and systematized the rhetorical techniques found throughout human cultures but first conceptualized by the Greeks (Kennedy 1984, 10-13). Aristotle and the later handbooks distinguished three types of speech. *Judicial* (or forensic) rhetoric belonged to the courtroom; it aimed to accuse or defend before a judge or jury. The purpose of *deliberative* rhetoric was to persuade a public assembly to take some action (or, conversely, to dissuade it from the same). Speakers used *epideictic* rhetoric on public memorial occasions to confirm communal values by praise or censure (Kennedy 1984, 19; Hansen 1989, 57; Mack 1990, 34).

Recent attention to the rhetorical aspects of Galatians is especially indebted to the pioneering work of Hans Dieter Betz (Betz 1974-75; Betz 1979). Betz classifies Galatians as an apologetic letter and thus an example of judicial rhetoric. It is Paul's self-defense against accusations by the agitators: "the addressees are identical with the jury, with Paul being the defendant, and his opponents the accusers" (1979, 24). Later, however, Betz seems to characterize Galatians as Paul's defense of the *Spirit* (Betz 1979, 25).

Although appreciative of Betz's contribution to the rhetorical analysis of Galatians, other scholars reject his claim that the letter is an example of judicial rhetoric. Particularly problematic for his theory is the parenesis (Gk. *parainesis*: moral advice or admonition) of 5:1–6:10, for the handbooks do not recognize exhortation as a feature of judicial rhetoric, as Betz himself realizes (Betz 1979, 254).

Others, then, find it more helpful to regard Galatians as an instance of deliberative rhetoric: Paul's aim is to persuade the Galatians to reject the appeal of the agitators (e.g., Kennedy 1984; Hall 1987; Smit 1989). Still others stress the difficulty of identifying Galatians with any single genre (Aune 1981, 325; Lyons 1985, 119, 173-75; Hansen 1989, 59). Concerned more with epistolary than rhetorical genre, Nils Dahl characterizes Galatians as a "mixed type" that evinces some notable affinities with private letters of rebuke and request (Dahl 1973). Pursuing Dahl's suggestion, Walter Hansen classifies Galatians as a "rebuke-request" letter, the rebuke consisting of 1:6–4:11 and the request, 4:12–6:10 (Hansen 1989, 27-54).

Such efforts to identify the rhetorical or epistolary genre of Galatians can easily give the impression that Paul composed this letter-speech with a handbook in hand, the features of one genre or another dictating its structure and strategy. That he did so is improbable. It is also unlikely that the recipients of the letter were concerned to identify its genre before hearing it. In its attempt to "overhear" Galatians, then, the present commentary leaves open the question of genre so as not to impose upon the letter an interpretive grid not available to its original hearers. I will nevertheless assume that Paul knew the speech and letter types of the handbooks and knew as well the conventional rhetorical techniques familiar to educated speakers and writers in his day, and I will note the three major types of "proof" or argument that Aristotle and later handbooks classify under the headings of *ethos* ("moral character"), *pathos* ("feeling," "emotion"), and *logos* ("word," "reason"). These three types correspond to three universal factors in any rhetorical situation: speaker or writer, audience, and discourse. An "ethical" proof aims to create confidence in the character of the speaker or writer—his credibility, reliability, trustworthiness. A "pathetic" proof plays on the emotions of hearers or readers, particularly by emphasizing the advantage (or, conversely, the disadvantage) of adopting a certain view. A "logical" proof emphasizes *ideas* and appeals to the experience and reason of hearers or readers (Kennedy 1984, 15-16). Galatians exhibits all three kinds of argument.

No matter how powerful the arguments that Paul devises in this letter, its impact depended in large measure on the skillfulness of its oral performance in the Galatian congregations. In the ancient world, an oral public reading was fraught with difficulties unfamiliar to us. Written documents lacked systematic punctuation and division into paragraphs or sentences, and in Greek manuscripts lines of letters were not even separated into individual words. Thus readers lacked visual clues to structure and meaning that we take for granted (Achtemeier 1990, 10-11). Can we infer from this state of affairs that Paul intended for the bearer of his letter to be as well its public reader and that this person was a trusted personal associate familiar with the apostle's thought—perhaps one of the "brothers with me" (1:2; NRSV paraphrases, "members of God's family") he mentions in the prescript, perhaps even the person who penned the letter? Would Paul expect such a person—acquainted with his state of mind and his purpose in writing—to "introduce" the letter, elaborate on its arguments, and answer questions from those present at its reading? Did the Galatians experience the letter *only* aurally, or did Paul's emissary carry several copies, leaving one with each congregation for further study and reflection? Finally, what response or range of responses, immediate and delayed, did the letter elicit? Not even the most learned scholar can answer such questions with anything more substantial than airy speculation. But questions that so clearly lack answers can have an important and salutary effect for modern readers of Galatians: they can remind us of our necessary ignorance, counter the scholarly inclination to claim too much, and help bridle an undisciplined curiosity that presses to know more than the available evidence will allow.

AUTHENTICITY AND DATE

Very few modern New Testament scholars have questioned the authenticity of Galatians. The letter's distinctive style, theological argument, and use of scripture support the firm consensus that the letter originated with the apostle Paul, whatever might have been the role of his amanuensis.

A similar consensus does not prevail regarding the date of Galatians. If Paul's conversion occurred c. 35 and the Jerusalem conference took place c. 48, all his letters probably date from 50 to 56 (Koester 1982, 2:103-104; Jewett 1979 [pull-out graph], who, however, dates the Jerusalem conference in 51). Most Pauline scholars agree that 1 Thessalonians is his earliest extant letter and Romans his latest, but where Galatians falls between these two cannot be ascertained. One bit of evidence may indicate that Paul wrote Galatians after 1 Corinthians. At 1 Cor 16:1, concerning the collection for the Jerusalem church that he is soliciting from his Gentile congregations, Paul writes: "You should follow the directions I gave to the churches of Galatia." We can infer from this that the apostle had given clear instructions to the Galatian churches regarding systematic contributions to the collection. His statement may imply that as he wrote 1 Corinthians he was still expecting to receive an offering from the Galatian congregations. At Rom 15:25-29, however, he mentions the contributions from Macedonia and Achaia but, strangely, says nothing about Galatia. (Nor does 2 Cor 8 or 9.) Why? Was the collection effort not successful in Galatia, and, if so, was that effort disrupted by the situation to which Paul is responding in his Galatian letter? However one answers these questions, juxtaposing 1 Cor 16:1 and Rom 15:25-29 yields the probability that Paul wrote Galatians between 1 Corinthians and Romans. He wrote 1 Corinthians from Ephesus, with his anticipated departure from that city already in view (1 Cor 16:5-8). If his Ephesian ministry lasted from approximately autumn 52 to spring 55 (Koester 1982, 2:104) and if he wrote Galatians after 1 Corinthians, Paul would have written Galatians in the mid 50s and not long before Romans. The available evidence, however, does not permit us to get beyond the uncertainty implicit in all the "ifs" of this paragraph. Paul's failure to mention Galatia in Rom 15:25-29 could have an explanation different from that proposed above.

COMMENTARY

THE PRESCRIPT (1:1-5)

Galatians begins with an epistolary prescript unremarkable in its basic pattern but nevertheless indicative of major emphases of the letter and unusual because of the doxology with which it ends.

Had Paul exactly followed the form of salutation conventional in the hellenistic letter of his day, he would have begun, "Paul and all the brothers with me, to the churches of Galatia, greetings!" This conventional form, however, he expands at two points: sender and greeting. His elaborations affirm the creative power of God and the saving work of Jesus Christ.

◊ ◊ ◊ ◊

With his "sender" statement, the opening words of the letter, Paul makes the first move in his strategy to gain the assent of his Galatian hearers: He sharply asseverates the basis of the authority that will underlie every claim and every argument that follows. He, *Paulus* (his Roman surname), is an *apostolos,* a commissioned and sent one, the delegate and representative of another. His standing as emissary he owes to no human source or instrumentality. His apostleship, and thus the authority he is now exercising *as* an apostle, is solely "through Jesus Christ and God the Father." By elaborating "Jesus Christ and God the Father" with the (Greek) participial phrase "who raised him from the dead," Paul emphasizes two points about the double source of his authority: the life-giving power of God and the unique status of Jesus.

The third word of Paul's Greek text is *not.* This resounding negative and its companion term *nor* (in the next phrase) are stern and emphatic. Later readers of all the Pauline letters can observe that, although he typically introduces himself as *apostolos,* Paul never elsewhere thinks it necessary to assert that he is *not* an apostle because of any human being. That he does so here is this letter's initial clue to one of his principal concerns: what the ultimate source of his authority and his gospel *is* and what it is *not.*

A second rhetorical ploy is Paul's insistence that his response to the Galatian situation is not idiosyncratic, not peculiar to him alone, for he claims as co-senders of the letter "all the brothers who are with me" (AT). Whether he thus refers to his coworkers in ministry, to other members of his missionary entourage, or (more generally) to fellow Christians in the city from which he writes is not clear. Nor need it be. The important point is that, having insisted on the divine origin of his apostleship, he now claims that he will not be articulating merely his own views. Hearers of the letter will soon learn that Paul writes (or dictates) in the first-person singular. Thus when he names "all the brothers with me" as his co-senders, he is not claiming that this letter is a committee effort but, rather, that others agree with the position he will be setting forth. We can infer that such agreement will have been the outcome of discussion among Paul and his associates. It would appear, then, that Galatians was not dashed off hastily and unreflectively.

The standard epistolary greeting, *chairein* ("greetings!"), Paul modifies to "grace *[charis]* to you and peace from God our Father and the Lord Jesus Christ." In the LXX the word *peace (eirēnē)* usually translates the Hebrew *shalom.* Sharing the Hebrew term's wide semantic range (from health and safety to contentment and tranquility), *eirēnē* refers not so much to an absence of war or conflict as to an encompassing well-being. The sense of blessing that it carries is particularly obvious in the greeting and leave-taking formulas "Peace be to (with) you" and "Go in peace" (e.g., Exod 4:18; Judg 6:23; 18:6; 19:20; 1 Sam 1:17; 20:42; 25:6; 2 Sam 15:9; 1 Kgs 5:19; 1 Chr 12:18; Dan 10:19; Tob 12:17.). In the LXX, *grace (charis)* appears most frequently in the expression "find grace [favor] before (or in the sight of) someone"; but the conceptual content of the term in the Pauline Jesus-communities is more akin to the Hebrew *chesed.* When used of God, this Hebrew word signifies the deity's saving help or gracious act of pardoning. In the overwhelming majority of cases, however, the LXX translates it "mercy" (NRSV: usually "steadfast love," "kindness," "loyalty") rather than "grace." Thus *charis* ("grace") seems to be a term more distinctive of the early Jesus-movement than of Diaspora Judaism.

Later readers can recognize the prescript's greeting as identical to that of Romans, 1 and 2 Corinthians, Philippians, and Philemon (1 Thessalonians has only "grace to you and peace"). In Paul's other letters, however, this greeting comes at the very end of the prescript, immediately before the beginning of the thanksgiving section that is typical of his letters. In Galatians, by contrast, the apostle expands the last phrase of the greeting ("[from] the Lord Jesus Christ") with a participial phrase (in the Greek) that reflects a widespread early Christian interpretation of Jesus' death: "who gave himself for our sins." To this phrase he adds a purpose clause: "so that he might rescue us out of the present evil age according to the will of our God and Father" (AT). Shaping Paul's language here is the apocalyptic notion of two ages inherited from certain circles of Judaism: the present age controlled by the powers of evil, and the future age of blessedness that, the Jesus-sect believed, God has inaugurated by raising Jesus from the dead. Exactly *how* Jesus' giving himself "for our sins" delivers persons out of the present evil age Paul does not here specify. His hearers can assume that in the letter-speech that follows he will clarify the nature and consequences of Christ's "rescue" from this age.

A final peculiarity of the Galatians prescript appears in the way it ends, on the emphatically theological note "to whom [i.e., to our God and Father] be the glory for ever and ever. Amen." In every other assuredly genuine Pauline letter the prescript ends with a greeting that invokes grace and peace upon the recipients. Only the Galatians prescript ends with a *doxology,* a doxology bound syntactically to the phrase "the will of our God and Father." The effect of ascribing eternal *glory* to the One whose *will* is being implemented by Jesus' efficacious death is to establish the firm *theo*logical parameters of everything that follows and, at the same time, subtly to reinforce the claim of verse 1 that the authority with which Paul writes derives ultimately from God. Furthermore, with a play on the word *age* (in v. 4 "the present evil age" and in v. 5 the standard phrase "into the ages of the ages" ["forever and ever" NRSV]) Paul underscores the contrast between the eternal horizon of the divine and the narrow environment that presently shapes human existence.

◊ ◊ ◊ ◊

The Galatians prescript provides modern readers their first indication of the symbolic world that Paul and the letter's original recipients share. With confessional language that an outsider would find puzzling, it adumbrates an unfolding drama decisive for human destiny, a drama into which Paul and the Galatian Christians are themselves caught up. The scriptwriter of this drama is God (note the stress on God's will at 1:4), who alone is worthy of eternal glory (1:5). But the script itself seems necessitated by a situation that is not as it should be, the life-world of humans that Paul calls "the present evil age." The major characters in this drama are the scriptwriter, God, conceived as powerful patron and *paterfamilias* ("God the Father," "our Father"); the Lord Jesus Christ, whose title-name designates him the anointed agent of the Father; the human beings who find voice in the confessional phrases "for our sins" and "our God and Father"; and, finally, Paul himself, whose special role derives from his being commissioned by Jesus Christ and God the Father. If we are to judge from the prescript, the central happenings of this drama are three. Two belong already to the past: the Lord Jesus Christ "gave himself for our sins" (1:4), and God the Father "raised him from the dead" (1:1). The third, in process or still in the future (the purpose clause of v. 4 leaves the point uncertain), is rescue from the life-world that is now humankind's home.

Three sharp antitheses mark Paul's letter opening: Jesus Christ and God the Father over against humans (1:1); resurrection versus death (1:1); and the "present evil age" in contrast to another life-world that *rescue* points to (1:4). A fourth lies half-concealed in the apostle's words: the will of God and whatever thwarts or impedes its realization. One begins to sense that such antitheses signal a perspective that will shape everything that follows.

BODY OF THE LETTER (1:6–6:10)

Paul's Steadfastness as an Apostle of Christ (1:6–2:21)

Modern commentators often divide Gal 1:6–2:21 into discrete parts, but the text itself signals no breaks. Various Greek particles (conjunctions and adverbs) bind the sentences of this section of the letter into a syntactically seamless whole. With respect to subject matter and types of statement, though, 1:6–2:21 is anything but homogeneous. It includes some statements specific to the epistolary situation, others that are general and thematic. More specifically, it includes a rebuke and the cause of that rebuke, an imprecation, a personal defense, accounts of personal experience, and a summary declaration about the gospel and its power in reshaping Paul's own life.

The opening passage of the section, 1:6-12, appears particularly heterogeneous, but the noun *gospel (euangelion)* and the corresponding verb *to proclaim the gospel (euangelizesthai)* provide an obvious coherence. In the long central "autobiographical" part of this section, Paul himself clearly marks crucial episodes of his personal history (save the first) with *then (epeita*, 1:18, 21; 2:1) or *but when (hote de*, 1:15; 2:11). The "speech" (2:15-21) that concludes the last of these episodes features a statement of Paul's understanding of the gospel and stresses his devotion as its bearer. This statement corresponds antithetically to the accusations and double *anathema* of 1:6-12 and, with that earlier passage, brackets the long "autobiographical" section of chapters 1 and 2. By introducing several new emphases of the letter ([works of] the Law, faith, justification), it also points ahead to the dense argument that will follow.

A Rebuke (1:6-10)

The "body" of a hellenistic letter often began with such conventional niceties as a wish for good health, assurance that the writer was making supplication to a deity on behalf of the addressee, or a statement of thanks to the gods for some favor. Typical of Paul's letters is a section (following the prescript) expressing such sentiments as his gratitude to God for the faith or love of the recipients or his remembrance of them and his longing to see them, the tone one of joy and confidence. Not so in Galatians. Here the "thanksgiving section" typical of Paul's letters is missing altogether. In its place the Galatians heard an unmistakable rebuke couched as an expression of surprise and amazement. We should be cautious, however, about taking Paul's "I am astonished . . . " as an ejaculation issuing solely from a certain psychological state. The Galatians will have heard *thaumazō* as a formula typical of a particular kind of hellenistic letter that aimed to effect some change in the recipient's behavior, often some act of negligence (such as a failure to write). The tone of such letters was one of disappointment and reproach, but often a note of confidence was obvious in an appeal to correct the offending conduct. If the bearer of Paul's letter had not already given a preliminary indication of the apostle's response to the Galatian situation, its recipients could no longer be in doubt when they heard his "I am astonished!" This exclamation told them that Paul was displeased and disappointed, and they now knew as well that they stood under his rebuke. They could now expect his letter to set forth the reason for his disapproval and his appeal for change.

The reason for his rebuke Paul declares at once: "You are so quickly deserting the one who called you in the grace of Christ" (some early manuscripts, lacking "of Christ," read: "the one who called you in grace"). The Galatians would know whether the reference point of "so quickly" was Paul's founding of the Galatian churches or Paul's departure from Galatia or the arrival of the agitators. We later readers cannot be sure. They could also know more surely than we what to make of the present tense of Paul's verb. The tense reflects, perhaps, a *process* that has already begun (and that Paul fears will continue). In any case, the subject of the verb ("you" rather than "*some* of you") suggests that he thinks of each of his congregations more as a *people* than as an aggregate of individuals. When used elsewhere in contexts where political or philosophical or religious allegiance is at issue, his verb means to change sides, to desert, or to become an apostate. Significantly, the apostle does not accuse the Galatians of changing from one understanding of the gospel to another. Rather, he says, they are deserting "the one who called you." Although Paul's expression (a participial phrase in Greek) is just ambiguous enough to remind his hearers of his own role in their conversion, it surely refers principally to God. In going over to an "other gospel" (Paul's term can mean either different in kind or simply another), they are not merely exchanging one set of ideas for another. Their defection is much more serious: in turning to a different gospel they are abandoning *God* and thus regressing to their state prior to grace.

Immediately upon mentioning the "different gospel" Paul corrects himself: "which is not another at all" (AT). The only sense in which there is "another gospel" is this: there are "some"—Paul employs the rhetorical device of dismissing these persons by referring to them in the most general manner possible—who are stirring up (or confusing) the Galatians and are wanting to change the gospel *(euangelion)* of Christ into something else. In the first-century political sphere *euangelion* was an imperial proclamation concerning the peace that Augustus brought the world. In the poems of Second Isaiah (LXX), the verb *euangelizesthai* refers to proclaiming the joyful news of God's salvation, the deity's deliverance of Israel from captivity in Babylon. In the Jesus-movement, "gospel" was already a technical term for the good news of what God was doing through the death and resurrection of Jesus. In Paul's view, though, a teaching that causes people to turn away from God and God's grace is not gospel. It is *not* good news.

In order now to stress how utterly unacceptable is the agitators' distortion of the gospel, Paul proceeds to demand their ouster from the Christian community. So certain is he of the truth of the gospel he initially preached to them that he calls down a curse upon himself, divinely commissioned though he is, or even upon one of God's heavenly messengers, if either of them were to preach a gospel other than what he had preached originally to the Galatians. ("We" rather than "I" is, of course, the subject of v. 8. This "we" may be merely the authorial plural equivalent to "I." More likely, however, the plural reflects historical actuality: on the occasion of founding the Galatian churches Paul had been not a lone operative but the leader of a missionary team.) For solemn emphasis the apostle exactly repeats his imprecation in verse 9: "Let that one be accursed!" In this repetition, however, he moves from the unreal, the barely imaginable ("even if *[ean]* we or an angel from heaven were to proclaim [subjunctive mood] to you a gospel other than . . . " [AT]) to the actual, the reality of the present situation: "if *[ei]* anyone is preaching [indicative mood] to you a gospel other than . . . " (AT). He also shifts from "what we proclaimed" to "what you accepted," thereby subtly reminding the Galatians of their earlier decision and underscoring the discrepancy between what they believed initially and what they are now hearing from the agitators.

The key term of Paul's imprecation, *anathema*, can mean, positively, a sacrifice or offering to God (2 Macc 2:13; 9:16; 3 Macc 3:17), but in the LXX it regularly translates the Hebrew *cherem*, something devoted to destruction. Deuteronomy 7:26 characterizes the *anathema* as a loathsome and abhorrent thing, an abomination, probably because it had previously been dedicated to an alien deity and was thus intolerable to Israel's God. In any case, the *anathema* was to be utterly destroyed, offered now as a sacrifice to the Lord (see *anathema* at Lev 27:28; Deut 13:17 [Heb 13:18]; Josh 6:17, 18; 7:1, 11, 12, 13; 22:20; 1 Chr 2:7; *anathēma* at Deut 7:26). It is in this specific sense that, in Paul's Bible, an *anathema* is a "cursed thing."

Several features of the texts just cited may be relevant for interpreting Gal 1:8-9. First, responsibility for destroying the thing "devoted to destruction" belonged to the people of Israel: it is they who are to offer the *anathema* to God. Second, the people's welfare depended on their fulfilling this responsibility (Deut 13:17 [Heb 13:18]; Josh 7). Third, according to Deut 7:26, anyone who brought an *anathema* into his house would himself become *anathema*, precisely the fate of Achan in Josh 7. In Gal 1:8-9 Paul does not demand that the agitators and their sympathizers be destroyed as a sacrifice to God. In light of the *anathema* passages in Deuteronomy and Joshua, however, I hold that he *is* pressing the Galatians to take responsibility for ridding the community of those persons who threaten their well-being, lest they too become displeasing to God. He is urging the Galatians to execute a curse of exclusion upon those who are stirring them up. The sharp contrast between "let him be *anathema*" and the "grace and peace" of the letter's greeting cannot fail to have struck Paul's hearers. That contrast leaves little doubt about how concerned the apostle is about the "other gospel" that threatens them. Nor would an astute hearer have missed the implied threat that his curse formula directs toward anyone considering yielding to the agitators' appeal.

Galatians 1:10 is a puzzle. Indeed, no other verse in the letter is more difficult to understand. It seems abruptly intrusive, and yet Paul's conjunction (Gk. *gar*, usually translated "for") indicates that, to his mind, it follows from, or is connected with, what he has just said. But what is the nature of that connection? Does "now" refer narrowly to the imprecation of verses 8-9, to the letter as a whole, or, even more generally, to Paul's whole apostolic ministry (note the implications of "still" in 10*c*)? Why does he append a statement to his second question but not to the first? And why is "or God" part of the first question but not the second?

Verse 10*bc*, Paul's second question and his own response to it, is the less difficult part of this verse. The apostle appears to acknowledge that at one time he *had* desired to please people (again, note "still"); but he insists that this is the case no longer, for such a motive would be incompatible with the loyalty required of him as a slave of Christ. Moreover, as the slave of a powerful master, he enjoys a status and authority that obviate any need to seek favors from human beings.

By, in effect, answering his own second question (10*c*), Paul leaves no doubt that he regards "pleasing people" as unacceptable. Unfortunately, he neither answers his first question (10*a*) nor provides any clues about how his hearers should respond. We cannot take verse 10*c* as a response to *both* questions because the absence of "or God" makes question two fundamentally different from the first. How the Galatians silently answered question one might have depended on whether they construed its "or" as copulative (virtually equivalent to "and") or disjunctive ("or rather"). These two different senses of the conjunction yield four possible responses to Paul's first question: (1) "obviously, Paul, you *are* trying to persuade both people and God"; (2) "of course you are not trying to persuade either people *or* God"; (3) "you are trying to persuade *people*, but not God"; (4) "you are trying to persuade not people but rather *God*."

In the view of many interpreters, the key to understanding Gal 1:10 is the *verb* of Paul's first question, *peithein*. Because its standard lexical meaning seems to make little sense here, some prefer to translate it as a near synonym of "to please," the verb in question two, thus "try to please, curry favor" or "seek approval" (so NRSV). But the use of this term in Greek and hellenistic literature does not allow great confidence in this move. No good reasons compel the interpreter to abandon the usual meaning of *peithein:* "to persuade"—that is, to win over, to prevail upon by argument or entreaty.

The question of verse 10*a* seems intrusive, interrupting the flow of thought between verses 8-9 and verse 11 (all three sentences feature the proclamation of the gospel). Why Paul would interrupt himself this way no one can say for sure, but it appears that he wishes to *respond* to something before he proceeds further. If the "now" of verse 10*a* refers primarily to verses 6-9, he could be anticipating the reaction his words might elicit among the letter's recipients. Does he have second thoughts about what he has just said? Might his language have been intemperate and altogether too harsh? Does he suspect the Galatians will complain about rhetorical overkill, especially in his pronouncing the *anathema* twice? Whatever the reasons for interjecting verse 10, we hear Paul asking: "What! Am I now trying to persuade human beings—or God?" (AT). One might indeed think so. Paul's double injunction, "let that one be accursed," is an overt attempt to prevail upon the Galatians to take a particular action. Moreover, his expression of shocked dismay (1:6) and his sharp accusations against the agitators (1:7) do not appear to be the devices of a rhetorical naif. Yet Paul surely knew that many thoughtful people regarded the "art of persuasion" with suspicion because of the ease with which rhetoric could be used to lie and deceive. As for "persuading" *God,* in a biblical-Jewish context a curse formula inevitably implies an appeal to the deity. Is Paul, then, acknowledging that he is trying to persuade people and God? He does not say, and perhaps we do well to *accept* his silence rather than fill it with our own speculations. He voices the *question,* thereby, perhaps, revealing something of his concern about how the Galatians might respond to his rhetoric; but he does not signal his hearers how he would himself answer if pressed to do so. Instead he deflects this question by at once raising another: "Am I trying to please people?" And no one can mistake his answer to that.

A Fundamental Claim (1:11-12)

Although Paul has omitted the conventional thanksgiving, has rebuked his hearers for turning to a "gospel" that is no gospel, has urged the expulsion of the agitators and has obliquely threatened the Galatians with a similar fate, he now addresses them, for the first time, as "brothers" (1:11). In Paul's world, "brother" could designate a fellow member of one's people or of some voluntary association. In using the term in the context of verses 6-12, however, the apostle seems to be deliberately if unobtrusively reminding his hearers that they and he belong to the same *family*, the family that God has summoned from out of the present evil age (recall "*called in grace*" at 1:6).

The link between 1:11 and 1:10 is the unspoken assertion implied by 10*c*—that is, "and I am certainly a slave of Christ." Paul's status as Christ's slave he grounds directly in the gospel he preaches. Actually, Paul speaks not of "the gospel I proclaim." He says, rather: "the gospel that was proclaimed by me." His passive construction serves to highlight the *gospel* and quietly relegate himself—who, in this letter, is pressing his apostolic authority to its limit—to a mere *instrument* of the divine purpose. That gospel, he insists, is by its very nature "not a human sort of thing" (AT). (NRSV's "not of human origin" conceals the fact that in the phrase *kata anthrōpon* [v. 11], the preposition *kata* conveys the notion of the distinctive nature, quality, or character of something.) Paul bases this claim on the peculiar way he received the gospel: he got it from no human being, nor was he taught it; rather, "through a revelation of Jesus Christ" (the missing verb to be supplied is probably "I received [it]"—so NRSV). His declaration, forceful as it is, raises the question: What, exactly, is he claiming to have received? A set of detailed propositions that God conveyed to him and that constituted the content of the gospel he preached? Such seems hardly conceivable. The principal conceptual lineaments of his gospel, then? Such seems only slightly less improbable. Paul characterizes the means by which he received the gospel as "a revelation of Jesus Christ." This revelation had confronted him with the inescapable reality, present and powerful, of the crucified one. From beyond the age of evil and death the living Christ appeared to him; and because of this undeniable, absolutely authoritative experience, Paul had no choice but to believe that the claim of the Nazarene's followers was, after all, true: God had raised Jesus from the dead. In the context of first-century Jewish apocalyptic expectations, Paul would have understood the resurrection of the Crucified One not as an isolated happening but as the beginning of the new age. Such is the "good news," the gospel, that he preached. In a way that he does not here detail, his vision of the risen Christ entailed the insight (at that moment? later?) that what God was doing in raising Christ embraced all of God's creation. This was the insight that impelled him to take the message of Christ crucified-and-raised to the Gentiles.

The point Paul presses home in 1:11-12 is this: The gospel he preaches does not have the character of a human construct. He did not formulate the gospel as the end product of a process of meditation and reflection. He claims, rather, that it intruded upon him, irrupting into his life from the domain of the divine. In the following passage he will briefly describe this revelation as an unexpected event of personal transformation. At greater length he will then recount several episodes demonstrating its consequences in his life as a slave of Christ and a faithful bearer of the gospel.

To stress the unexpectedness of Paul's revelation is not to say that nothing had prepared him for it. But what? His letters include no evidence that he had been burdened by a sense of guilt because of an inability to comply perfectly with God's Law. A provocative suggestion is that what had prepared him was an internal conflict between a vision of the oneness of humanity (nurtured by universalist tendencies in biblical writings and in hellenism) and his commitment to the "ethnocentric" Law that made Jews a people apart (Boyarin 1994, 39, 59, 107).

Paul's Call to Apostleship (1:13-17)

To underscore the startling reversal effected by the revelation of Jesus Christ, Paul describes the person he was just prior to that happening (1:13-14). Most notably, he twice uses the term *Judaism* to name the religious community that had shaped him. The community of Jesus-people he designates "the church *[ekklēsia]* of God." In the LXX the *ekklēsia* is the "assembly" of Israel, those members of the people "called out" and gathered together to worship, to fight, to make some important decision, to hear the word of the Lord on some special occasion. That Paul now calls the community he had once tried to destroy "the church of God" bespeaks dramatically the life transformation that he wishes to highlight. How he now conceives the relationship between "Judaism" and "the church of God" is a complicated issue, but his language here suggests that the Jesus-community is the true people of God. The *church [ekklēsia]* of God is those people, Jew and Gentile, whom God has *called [kalein]* in grace.

If, as is likely, "you have heard" (1:13) alludes to Paul's initial preaching and teaching among the Galatians, this and subsequent verses constitute a *reminder;* and a reminder of some past happening shared by two parties can have the subliminal effect of strengthening a bond or renewing a relationship. More obviously, these verses function to portray Paul as an expert in the Law and traditions of Israel, a man of intense conviction who surpassed his contemporaries in his religious zeal, and, not least, a man whose convictions led to *action.* He was not, he insists, a mere Sabbath Jew. Apparently, though, he does not think it relevant to explain *why* his zeal for his ancestral traditions impelled him to persecute the church and try to destroy it. He finds it sufficient to stress that he *did,* and that he did so *kath' hyperbolēn,* "to the limit" (NRSV: "violently"). Against the background of such a manner of life as this, Paul's revelation and the way it played itself out in his subsequent conduct shine all the more brightly.

The phrase "but when" (1:15) marks the momentous shift from Paul's pre-revelation to his post-revelation life. No one can say how closely his account in verses 15-16 of the "revelation of Jesus Christ" (1:12) corresponds to the account he might have offered immediately after the event. Later experience and present epistolary situation must surely affect what he writes here. He says that the source of the revelation was God and its "subject" was God's son.

He affirms that this revelation was the means by which God implemented a prior divine decision, for, he says, God "had set me apart before I was born and called me through his grace." The revelation of God's son was a moment in the unfolding of the divine plan for humankind. Paul's language (literally: "who appointed me from my mother's womb") may suggest not merely that God had him "under contract" from the moment of his birth but also that the very reason for his being born was to become the apostle of Christ. The collocation of the word *womb* and the notion of being set apart (or appointed) for a task is reminiscent of Jer 1:5, and *womb* and God's *calling* appear conjointly in Isa 49:1. The echo of Jer 1 and Isa 49 appears to be deliberate, for both texts also mention a mission of God's chosen one to the nations/Gentiles (*ethnē* at LXX Isa 49:6; Jer 1:5, 10). Paul seems to regard himself as the latter-day successor of Jeremiah and the prophetic "slave of the Lord" (see *doulos* at LXX Isa 49:3, 5 and at Gal 1:10), like them called and appointed to be God's envoy to the Gentiles *(ethnē)*. Clearly, then, Paul understood (or came to understand) his experience as a commissioning by God of the prophetic type. It is also appropriate, however, to call his experience a conversion. To be sure, he does not describe a turning from a life of sin to one of godliness, nor does he give any indication that he felt the lifting of a burden of guilt. But the man was obviously transformed. The change from persecutor of the church to fervent preacher of the gospel admits of no other explanation.

What the apostle means by designating Jesus God's *son* (1:16) might have been clear to the Galatians on the basis of his earlier preaching. In Paul's Bible and theirs, the LXX, God's son is variously Israel (e.g., Exod 4:22; Hos 11:1), the Davidic king (e.g., 2 Sam 7:14; Ps 2:7), or the righteous Israelite (e.g., Sir 4:10; Wis 2:18); and "son" in each case points to a relationship with God of special intimacy, responsibility, or faithfulness. Students of the New Testament still debate, though, whether Paul's Christology included belief in the preexistence of the Son. On the basis of *this* letter, all one can confidently say is that the apostle regarded God's son as the anointed one *(Christos)* whom God raised from the dead (1:1).

God was pleased to reveal his son *en emoi,* writes the apostle. The preposition *en* can have an instrumental sense ("by means of"), but that meaning ill fits the present context because "revealed his son through me" would then be equivalent to "preach him among the Gentiles" in the following clause. That clause, however, declares the *purpose* of God's revealing his son, an event prior to and preparatory to Paul's preaching among the Gentiles rather than identical with that preaching. *En emoi* must therefore mean "in me," Paul's emphasis being on the personal subjective character of the experience, or something like "in my particular case." "Who called (me) through his grace" echoes "who called you in grace" at 1:6 and stresses God's purpose and initiative. In that earlier verse, though, Paul charges that those who were called were deserting God. At 1:15 he is beginning to make the case that he, by contrast, has been steadfastly obedient to God's call.

God revealed his son, Paul writes, "so that I might proclaim him among the Gentiles." Note that he does not claim that the revelation itself included verbal instructions from God to preach to the Gentiles. Paul's "so that" clause conceals more than it discloses. It declares the *purpose* of God's revelation, but it does not clarify how or when Paul became aware of that divine purpose.

Many readers of Paul's letters find the importance of Gal 1:15-17 in the meager details these verses provide about his life-changing "religious experience." Everything that the apostle says about his call and its purpose, however, falls in an introductory *subordinate* clause. The syntax of his sentence throws his stress not on his conversion experience itself but on how he *responded* to that happening, what he did immediately thereafter. He did not right away confer with any human being ("flesh and blood"), he says, nor did he go up to Jerusalem to (be with) those who were apostles before he was. Instead he went away into Arabia and returned again to Damascus. That he "returned" to Damascus strongly implies that his revelation had occurred in that city or its environs. "Arabia" designates not the huge peninsula lying between the Red Sea and the Persian Gulf but, probably, the desert kingdom of Nabatea to the south of Damascus (and south and southeast of the Dead Sea).

It is difficult to resist the urge to speculate about Paul's reasons for going to "Arabia." Does he go to preach the gospel there? Although this section of the letter focuses on his uncompromising faithfulness to the divine will, he does not say so. By emphasizing that he did *not* right away confer with "flesh and blood," is he implying in verses 16-17 that he went into Arabia to confer with *God*—that is, to think through, with divine guidance, the implications of what had happened to him? How long did he remain in Arabia, and why did he return to Damascus? No one can say, and the answers to such questions do not fall within the range of the apostle's present aim. What he stresses is this: after God's revelation of his son he did not confer with anyone, not even those leaders of the Jerusalem "mother church" whom he acknowledges were already apostles before he was. What he did *not* do speaks powerfully of the absolute authority of his revelation experience.

A Visit with Cephas (1:18-24)

"Then" (1:18) marks another episode whose recounting is germane to Paul's present purpose: after three years (whether from his revelation or from his return from Arabia to Damascus must remain uncertain) he did finally go to Jerusalem. He went "to visit Cephas" (the root meaning of the Greek verb is "to inquire or examine"). The Aramaic *Kephas* is the exact equivalent of the Greek *Petros,* the two names a play on the word *rock* in each language; "Cephas" is thus Simon Peter. Paul's infinitive of purpose in verse 18 gives the impression that it was he who took the initiative in going to Jerusalem, but he does not explain why he went when he did. And although "stayed with him" implies that he was Cephas's houseguest, he does not recount what they talked about during his visit. One can easily imagine that Jesus of Nazareth, Cephas's Easter experience (see e.g., Luke 24:34; 1 Cor 15:3-5), and the beginnings of the Jesus-movement were among the matters Paul wished to learn about, but we do well not to confuse what seems plausible to us with what actually happened. Here is one of the many places we must be willing to live with our necessary ignorance.

Since Paul stayed with Cephas for fifteen days—a period that would have twice included "the first day of the week," the day of

Christian assembly and worship—it is remarkable that he did not even "see" any other apostle except James, the brother of Jesus. Whether his lack of contact with any other apostle was deliberate he does not say. He does, however, think it necessary precisely at this point to take an oath: "In what I am writing to you, before God, I do not lie!" (1:20). Why this "sworn testimony"? Was Paul aware of different versions of his first Jerusalem visit that he must now counter? Whatever the reason, the distinction in verses 18-19 between what he freely acknowledges and what he denies is striking. He probably would not go out of his way to note that he was with Cephas for fifteen days if (as some hold) the purpose of these verses was to counter the charge that he had acquired his gospel in Jerusalem. What he underlines with an oath is the number of people he had contact with: he got to know Cephas and he "saw" James, but he had *no* contact with any other apostle. It would have been impossible, then, for the leaders of the Jesus-movement in Jerusalem to have commissioned Paul or, as an official body, to have otherwise legitimized what he was doing in Damascus. Thus he is insisting in verses 19-20 that nothing happened in Jerusalem that in any way threatened either his independence or the sole sufficiency of God's revelation to him.

With a second "then" at 1:21 Paul marks his years in the territories of Syria and Cilicia as another significant period of his life as an apostle. His aim is not, however, to tell anything about the nature or results of his ministry. His sole emphasis is on his reputation in Judea during the extended period of his work in Syria and Cilicia. He was "unknown by sight" (literally: "by face") to the Christian congregations in Judea; the members of those congregations were, however, hearing *about* him, hearing that the former persecutor was now "proclaiming the faith he once tried to destroy." Not only were they aware of his personal transformation, their typical reaction (imperfect verb tense: "they were glorifying") was to give glory to God *en emoi*, "in my case," that is, because of Paul's about-face. This echo of Paul's earlier doxology (1:5) is not accidental. At the end of the Galatians prescript, between a statement about the will of God and Paul's rebuke of the Galatians for deserting God, the apostle had ascribed glory *(doxa)* to God "forever and ever." Now he is at pains to note that his transformation from persecutor to evangelizer was cause for the Judean churches to glorify God (the verb is *doxazein*). Thus does he remind his hearers of his key role in the divine plan.

It is noteworthy that at 1:23 Paul characterizes the Christian message as "the faith." That he (or, earlier, the Judean Christians) could so designate the Christian proclamation of the Crucified and Risen One bears two important implications: first, the term *pistis* could usefully serve as a summary characterization of the Christian message; because it is not a key term in the religious vocabulary of the LXX or hellenistic Jewish writings and thus did *not* serve to characterize Judaism, *faith* points us to a distinctive feature of the early Jesus-movement. Second, the multiple connotations of *pistis*—being persuaded, believing, having confidence in, relying on, trusting, being committed to, being faithful—suggest that being identified with the Jesus-movement required deliberate decision that distanced persons from the socio-religious world that had heretofore provided their identity, whether Jewish or "pagan."

Paul Presents His Gospel in Jerusalem (2:1-10)

Once again, at 2:1, "then" marks the beginning of a new episode. That Paul's account of his second journey to Jerusalem is the lengthiest in the "autobiographical" section attests its key importance to the letter's purpose.

"After fourteen years" could indicate the lapse of time since Paul's call experience. More likely (more likely because of the wording "I went up again"), he means fourteen years since his first visit to Jerusalem. He says he went with Barnabas, but with the verbs and participle of verses 1 and 2 (Paul is the grammatical subject of all seven of them) he gives the unavoidable impression that the journey was *his* project. He does assert, of course, that he went up "in response to a revelation," but he leaves that phrase tantalizingly vague. His earlier use of the noun *revelation* (1:12) and the verb *reveal* (1:16) makes clear both the source (God) and the "content" (Jesus Christ) of his life-changing experience. Here, though, he indicates nothing at all about the nature of the revelation that prompted (or reinforced) his decision to go to Jerusalem, and he relies solely on the *word* (the word *revelation*) to imply that the ultimate agent on this occasion was God. Verse 2 provokes the first of many questions that this passage raises but does not answer: Was this revelation a private one, to Paul alone, or was it given through a prophet to a Christian assembly in Antioch? Were Paul and Barnabas (and perhaps Titus) an official delegation sent by the Antioch church to Jerusalem; and if so, was the sending of this delegation prompted by issues troubling the Christian community there? Paul's wording in v. 2 (in Greek his conjunction is *and*, not *then*) implies, without stating, some connection between the revelation and his setting forth the gospel he preached among the Gentiles. What was the nature of that connection? And why that presentation in a private meeting with only the three leading apostles? Again, silence.

Paul's language does not support the view that he presented his gospel before the whole assembly ("them" in v. 2*a*) and then met privately with James, Cephas, and John. The conjunction *de* at verse 2*b* is explanatory: I laid before them the gospel—that is, in a private meeting. Had Paul wanted to describe two separate occasions, his intent would have been clearer had he used an expression such as "all of them" (see 2:14) to correspond to "in a private meeting"; and one would expect at least the less ambiguous conjunction *kai* ("and").

Whether or not the "revelation" was the sole reason for Paul's second trip to Jerusalem, he clearly states his reason for laying his gospel before "them": "in order to make sure that I was not running, or had not run [that is, in past years of his Gentile ministry], in vain." Here Paul uses the metaphor of running, as in a race, to suggest his dedication and exertion as a slave of Christ. But what does he mean by *eis kenon*, "in vain"? And what response from the Jerusalem apostles would satisfy him that he had not worked in vain? Conversely, what would convince him that he *had*? What, exactly, is he uncertain about, and what, after fourteen years, has caused his unease? Some change of attitude on the part of influential Christian Jews? Certain behaviors or some event among his Gentile converts? Somehow the question of whether his work had been for nought appears to be directly related to the gospel he set before the principal leaders of the Jerusalem church. What feature of that gospel, then, was at issue, potentially capable of rendering his missionary work futile?

Having stated the purpose of presenting his gospel in Jerusalem, Paul does not at once proceed to note the apostles' response (that comes only in v. 6). What he says instead is this: Titus was not compelled to be circumcised. Actually, Paul's statement in verse 3 is considerably fuller. He says: "But even Titus, who was with me, was not compelled to be circumcised, though he was a Greek." The word *but (alla)* implies that the question of circumcision was *the* prominent issue in Paul's presentation of his gospel: I set before them the gospel I preach, *but* Titus was not compelled to be circumcised. Paul had just informed the hearers of this letter that he and Barnabas took Titus with them to Jerusalem, so "who was with me" might indicate that Titus was present not merely in Jerusalem but in the private meeting as well. Paul's "even," however, might give "who was with me" a different force: if Titus, who was *with* me, was not compelled to be circumcised, then neither would any other Christian Gentile have to undergo circumcision, Titus being the test case. Furthermore, the note that Titus was a Greek does not merely convey the information that it states (i.e., that Titus was a non-Jew); it, too, points to the issue responsible for Paul's concern: the status of uncircumcised Gentiles in the Jesus-movement, Christian Gentiles who had not become Christian Jews.

In light of Gal 1:1, 11-12, 13-14, it is hardly conceivable that Paul went to Jerusalem because he was troubled by any uncertainty about the substance of his gospel message or missionary practice, a practice based on the conviction that because of Jesus' death and resurrection Gentiles need not—*must* not!—become Jews (be circumcised) in order to belong to the people of God. No, Paul was by no means uncertain about the *truth* of his gospel. He was uncertain, rather, about its effect and consequences. He was concerned about a matter that lay outside his control and had little to do with the gospel's truth. His concern, I suggest, was this: Did the Jerusalem mother church understand that there was but one people of God and did they understand that the bond that unified that one people was Messiah Jesus and Messiah Jesus alone? If the leaders of the Jerusalem church did not agree with this conviction, if they were prepared to insist that Gentiles had to become Jews in order to belong to God's end-time people, then Paul's missionizing work would be proved futile. Why so? If Paul knew that Gentiles *were* God's people because of Christ, why did it matter whether Jerusalem acknowledged that truth or not? The answer must be that the opinion of the Jerusalem church leaders would have *practical* consequences for his evangelizing efforts. Were they to insist on circumcision for Gentile converts, Paul's Law-free Gentile mission would have been considerably undermined, especially among Gentile God-fearers who would be inclined to take Jerusalem's view very seriously.

The syntactical precision that has marked Galatians to this point gives way to two anacolutha (abrupt mid-sentence shifts to a different grammatical construction) in verses 4-6 that make following Paul's train of thought difficult. He describes the "false brothers" as "brought in," and the verb from which this verbal adjective is formed sometimes has the connotation of bringing in secretly or as part of some conspiracy. But *who* brought these people in, and for what purpose? Were they "brought in" by the leading apostles themselves? Certainly they must have been present with at least the apostles' *permission*. Does the conspiracy connotation of "brought in" imply that these persons intruded into the private meeting without the prior agreement of all parties? Where were they "brought in" *from*? Were they citizens of Jerusalem? Were they people who had dogged Paul during his Syria-Cilicia ministry and who had now, without Paul's prior knowledge, been (re)called to Jerusalem to give *their* account of that ministry? Paul says that they came in (or, perhaps, slipped or sneaked in) "to spy on the freedom we have in Christ Jesus, so that they might enslave us" (2:4). Exactly what he means by "spy" is far from clear. To "spy on" is to observe secretively for the purpose of gathering information, but persons "brought in," and thus *present,* would not be observing covertly. "Spy on," then, might say more about the pseudo-brothers' hostile intentions than their visibility or mode of operation. Indeed, the numerous questions that Paul's account leaves unanswered suggest that his aim here is not so much to present factual information as to disparage those persons at the Jerusalem conference who are, in his mind, prototypes of the Galatian agitators.

In spite of the anacoluthon of verse 4 it is natural to take the persons of 5a (to whom, Paul says, "we did not submit . . . even for a moment") as the "false brothers" and would-be enslavers of verse 4. Thus verses 4-5 are best understood as a brief elaboration of the attempt implied by verse 3, the attempt to have Titus circumcised. Paul says that he resisted this effort "so that the truth of the gospel might remain for you" (2:5 AT). He can hardly mean that he took the stance that he did in Jerusalem solely for the sake of the Galatian Christians. "You," then, is inclusive—the Galatians as members of a class, *all* Gentile believers. Even so, Paul's "you" reminds the Galatians that they are the beneficiaries of his (and Barnabas's) unyielding steadfastness as a defender of the gospel and a slave of Christ.

In verses 3-6 Paul has focused on his (and Barnabas's) resistance to the ploys of the pseudo-brothers who challenged the Law-free gospel in Jerusalem. In verse 6 he finally reports the response of the Jerusalem leaders to his presentation of the gospel he preaches among the Gentiles: They did not lay anything else upon him; that is, as verses 3-5 have already intimated, they did not insist that he modify his missionary practice or the gospel he had been preaching. To the contrary, he reports, the "pillar" apostles gave to him and Barnabas the right hand of fellowship, a ritual act of agreement "that we to [or for] the Gentiles and they to [or for] the circumcision" (2:9 AT); the verb to be supplied perhaps is *should go* (so NRSV) or *should preach* (or perhaps, on the pattern of v. 8, one might render: "that we would be apostles to the Gentiles and they, apostles to the circumcision"). A glance at the text will reveal that Paul's statement of results is hardly as laconic as the sentences above would suggest. Indeed, he accounts for the leaders' decision in three separate expressions, the second related to the first as an explanatory parenthesis: (1) "when they perceived that I had been entrusted with the gospel of the uncircumcision just as Peter [had been entrusted with the gospel] of the circumcision" (2:7 AT); (2) "for the one who worked through Peter for an apostleship of the circumcision worked also through me for the Gentiles" (2:8 AT);

(3) "and when they became aware of the grace given to me" (2:9 AT).

Notable in verses 7-8 is the non-Pauline language ("gospel of the uncircumcision [literally: foreskin]" and "gospel of the circumcision"; "Peter" instead of "Cephas"), which may reflect the actual language of the Jerusalem agreement. More pertinent to Paul's *purpose* is the observation that each of the "reasons" he gives in verses 7-9 stresses *God's* initiative in granting him a mission and an authority equivalent to Peter's, although God is, semantically, behind the scenes. *God,* in other words, does not appear as a grammatical subject, yet clearly it is God who has entrusted the gospel to Paul, it is God who has worked through Paul for the Gentiles, and it is God who has empowered Paul with grace.

Paul says that James, Cephas, and John, presumably at the Jerusalem conference, discerned that grace which had been given to him. What enabled them to perceive that God had indeed entrusted to Paul the "gospel of the foreskin"? Was the evidence that persuaded them empirical, Paul's undeniable success in making Gentile converts? Was it the testimony of Barnabas (and, perhaps, Titus)? Was it his own account of his Christ-revelation? Was it his (and Barnabas's) effective response to the arguments of the pseudo-brothers? The apostle, of course, does not say.

The right hand of fellowship sealed one further agreement: that, although their missionary responsibility concerned the Gentiles, Paul and Barnabas would nevertheless remember the poor, presumably the poor of Palestine or, more narrowly, Jerusalem. The verb *remember* here carries overtones of solicitude and beneficence. Some interpreters have held that "the poor" could be a self-designation attesting the Christian community's piety and eschatological consciousness (see 1QpHab 12.2-6). More likely, "the poor" has a quite literal reference. The "pillar" apostles' request becomes all the more understandable if the Jerusalem conference took place in 48 CE or shortly thereafter, because a famine mentioned by Josephus (*Ant.* 20 §51) befell Palestine in that year or, perhaps, a year or two earlier. In light of the numerous details about the Jerusalem conference that are *missing* in Gal 2:1-10, why does Paul include *this* one, the request to remember the poor? And why does he stress his eagerness to comply? If the Galatians had been negligent in contributing to Paul's collection for Jerusalem from his Gentile churches, as a comparison of 1 Cor 16:1-4 with Rom 15:25-27 seems to suggest (in the later [Romans] text Paul says nothing about the Galatians!), the Galatians might well hear 2:19 as a tacit rebuke. In any case, Paul here presents an image of himself as gracious and cooperative, eager to contribute to the welfare of fellow Christian Jews.

In his account of the Jerusalem conference Paul makes several significant claims. First, Titus was not compelled to be circumcised; by implication, then, the Jerusalem leaders acknowledged that *all* male Christian Gentiles were free of this requirement. Second, Paul (and Barnabas) did not yield to the pseudo-brothers; they refused to be "enslaved," refused to surrender the freedom they claimed as Christians. Third, the Jerusalem leaders "laid nothing in addition on me" (NRSV: "contributed nothing to me"); they did not try to force Paul to alter his gospel or his missionary practice. To the contrary, they sanctioned his Gentile mission. Paul makes a particularly noteworthy claim in the purpose clause of verse 5: He resisted the pseudo-brothers in order to defend and preserve the "truth of the gospel."

Even as he makes these claims, however, Paul at the same time acknowledges that he did, after all, go to Jerusalem to lay his gospel before the recognized leaders of the Jesus-movement; he admits, in effect, that their approval was somehow essential to the effectiveness of his Gentile mission. This admission would appear to rest somewhat uneasily alongside his central claim that his gospel, his apostleship, and his apostolic authority come from God and God alone. One recalls that in his depiction of his antagonists at the Jerusalem conference Paul resorts to name-calling ("false brothers," "slipped in," "spy," "enslave"). His more nuanced portrayal of the leading Jerusalem apostles reflects the ingenious rhetorical strategy by which he manages the apparent contradiction between his commissioning by God alone and his need for Jerusalem's approval.

His strategy (conscious or unconscious) is to grant full presence to the Jerusalem leaders only gradually, finally naming them only in 2:9. At 2:2 he says vaguely that he presented "to them" the gospel that he preached among the Gentiles. Oddly, "them" has no antecedent, to this point Paul having stated only that he went up "to Jerusalem." Immediately, however, he recounts that he met privately with *tois dokousin*. This phrase means, literally, "the ones who seem" or "those reputed," but in Greek literature the expression sometimes has a distinctly positive connotation: esteemed persons, persons of high reputation. I propose that Paul is deliberately exploiting the expression's potential for ambiguity (those who [merely] seem/persons highly esteemed), a semantic ambiguity that corresponds nicely with his ambivalence toward (and relationship with) the Jerusalem apostles. In 2:6, which is another anacoluthon ("*from* those . . . they laid nothing in addition on me"), "the ones reputed" become "the ones reputed to be something" (NRSV: "those who were supposed to be acknowledged leaders"), but then Paul adds immediately, "whatever sort [of people] they were (NRSV: what they actually were) makes no difference to me. God shows no partiality." (The Greek wording, "God does not take a person's face," renders literally a Hebrew idiom [found, e.g., at Lev 19:15; Job 13:8, 10; Ps 82:2; Prov 18:5] that probably referred originally to someone lifting the head of a person bowed or prostrate as a sign of favor—an act that, in its negative form, became a metaphor for the impartial judgment of God or righteous judges.) By implication, Paul is claiming that he bases his own refusal to grant the Jerusalem apostles superior authority on nothing less than the impartiality of God! It is hard to resist the impression that, in his insistence that "whatever sort they were" makes no difference, the apostle doth protest too much. If their status and authority were indeed matters of indifference to him and to the Galatians, verse 6bc would have no point or purpose.

In 2:9 Paul becomes even more specific about the "them" of 2:2, finally *naming* his conferees and acknowledging that James, Cephas, and John were "reputed to be (NRSV: acknowledged) pillars," that is, the principal and foundational authorities of the Jesus-movement. By delaying their full presence until this point, however, he has already indirectly challenged any claim that their status and authority overshadow his own and has forcefully affirmed that his no-circumcision mission is equally as valid as Peter's.

A Confrontation in Antioch (2:11-14)

The tone of Paul's self-presentation and of his narrative changes abruptly as he turns to the last episode of the letter's autobiographical section, the incident at Antioch. A semantic signal alerts his hearers that the nature and consequences of the happening in Antioch differed significantly from the events he has previously described. The word *epeita* ("then," "after that") introduces his account of his first visit to Jerusalem (1:18), his Syria-Cilicia ministry (1:21), and the Jerusalem conference (2:1). "Then" is conspicuously missing at 2:11. Instead we hear, "*But when* Cephas came to Antioch. . . . " And this Cephas is no longer the "pillar" whom Paul, years earlier, had visited for fifteen days and who, with James and John, had offered Paul the right hand of fellowship in token of his approval of Paul's Gentile mission. Now Cephas becomes the principal target of his wrathful indignation, and Paul's description of Cephas's conduct and his motives becomes truculent and judgmental. In Antioch, he says, he resisted (or opposed) Cephas "to his face" because he was "condemned." Condemned by whom he does not specify. Perhaps he means that Cephas had condemned himself by his behavior (so NRSV: "self-condemned"). Perhaps he implies that Cephas's behavior stood under *God's* judgment. In any case, he accuses Cephas of acting out of fear. In charging the rest of the Christian Jews with *joining* him in playing the hypocrite, and in addressing him alone (v. 14), Paul makes Cephas, in effect, the instigator of the "hypocrisy" that consumed all the Jewish members of the Antioch congregation. His most intense disappointment, though, was the conduct of his co-missioner: "even Barnabas was carried away [NRSV: led astray] by their hypocrisy" (2:13). The root meaning of Paul's verb *synhypokrinesthai* and noun *hypokrisis* is to play the part of another, like an actor on stage, and thus to pretend. Cephas and the others were acting disturbingly out of character. The metaphor of 2:14 further illuminates the reason for Paul's indignation: He realized, he says, that Cephas, Barnabas, and the other Christian Jews "were not walking straight in accord with [or toward] the truth of the gospel" (AT), and he presents himself as the sole Christian Jew in Antioch who unwaveringly stayed the course.

As Paul describes his confrontation with Cephas, the situation was this: before "certain people from James" came to Antioch, Cephas was sharing meals with Christian Gentiles as a matter of course. This meal sharing carried distinct symbolic meaning: it had the effect of declaring that Cephas did not allow the dietary strictures of Torah or the customs of Judaism to bar him from full acceptance of, and open communion with, Gentile members of the Jesus-people. Whether "certain people from James" were officially delegated representatives of James or persons who came with his blessing or merely persons who identified themselves with his views, no one can say. But upon their arrival Cephas "started withdrawing, keeping himself apart" (NRSV: "drew back and kept himself separate," but the imperfect verbs suggest that his behavior was not a dramatic act on one particular occasion but a pattern that emerged as he responded, perhaps, to pressure from the "people from James"). Paul charges that Cephas began avoiding table fellowship because he feared "those of the circumcision" (NRSV: "the circumcision faction"). This phrase probably has a wider sense than "certain people from James," referring to Jews (whether Christian or non-Christian) upset by what they regarded as the unprincipled admission of Gentiles into the full privileges of God's people. Verse 13 ("joined him in this hypocrisy") strongly implies that all the Christian Jews of Antioch followed Cephas's example, thereby marking the Gentiles as a distinct and separate part of the Christian community. This situation Paul found intolerable. It convinced him that the Christian Jews of Antioch had veered away from "the truth of the gospel." And because so much was at stake, it required him to confront Cephas before the whole Christian assembly.

According to Paul's recounting, the question he posed to Cephas was this: "If you, Jew that you are, live in a Gentile manner and not in a Jewish manner, how is it that you compel the Gentiles to Judaize?" (2:14 AT). To "live in a Gentile manner" means to disregard the requirements of Torah that identified Jews as a distinct and holy people (see Exod 19:5-6), and in the present context one thinks particularly of the laws concerning food and its proper preparation (Lev 11; 27:10-14; Deut 12:16, 23-24; 14). At this remove, however, Paul's question to Cephas is puzzling because of the present tense of the verb *live*. "You *live* in a Gentile manner"—after *withdrawing* from table fellowship with Gentiles? In view of the behavior that Paul finds so objectionable, one might expect *this* question instead: "If you, Jew that you are, were [earlier] living in a Gentile manner, how is it that you [now] compel Gentiles to Judaize?" The present tense of the verb *live* perhaps implies that in other regards, table fellowship with Gentiles excepted, Cephas was even now living "in a Gentile manner." Or perhaps the verb's tense does not bear its normal temporal reference. In that case Paul would be disregarding the "when" of Cephas's behavior and posing a rhetorical question that asserts a principle: You cannot live in a Gentile manner *and* yet compel Gentiles to Judaize. How Cephas's withdrawing from table fellowship was "compelling" Gentiles to adopt a Jewish way of life is also not clear, nor can one assume that Cephas intended to do that. Paul likely means that Cephas's behavior indirectly pressured Christian Gentiles to comply with Jewish food laws and customs because their refusal to comply would exclude them from full fellowship with their Jewish co-religionists.

Paul seems to be challenging Cephas's behavior primarily because of its effect on Christian Gentiles, but the implications of his stance for Christian Jews are also apparent. His condemnation of Cephas's withdrawal amounts to a demand that Christian Jews continue to eat with Gentiles even though continued table fellowship would mean abandoning the observance of Torah laws and Jewish custom. In effect, then, Paul was insisting that Cephas and Barnabas and the other Christian Jews make themselves Gentiles. When the oneness of God's new inclusive Israel was at stake, Paul would have *everyone* be Gentile!

We can be certain that Cephas would have objected vigorously to the way Paul characterizes his behavior and his motives in Antioch. But Paul's aim is not to provide the Galatians a balanced account of what happened and why. He never reports the outcome of his confrontation with Cephas. He does not claim that he changed anyone's mind, and his silence implies that, in fact, he did not. But the apostle seems little concerned that all the Christian Jews, even Barnabas, sided with Cephas. Indeed, he seems to revel in the fact that in Antioch he stood alone, distanced not only from the apostle he had visited years earlier, the apostle who had, with James and John, approved his Gentile mission with the right hand of fellowship, but also from his closest co-missioner. His recounting of the incident at Antioch amounts, again, to a self-portrait: Paul, abandoned even by coworker and by fellow apostle, but in spite of everything the resolute and uncompromising defender of the truth of the gospel.

"Not by Works of the Law" (2:15-21)

To ask whether 2:15-21 is a continuation of Paul's response to Cephas in Antioch or a statement formulated especially for the Galatians is to pose a false alternative. The passage is certainly aimed at the Galatians, and yet nothing in the text signals any break between 2:14 and 2:15. Furthermore, although the phrase can, by extension, include other Christian Jews as well, "we ourselves . . . Jews by birth" refers most naturally to Paul and Cephas. That Paul couches verses 15-21 as his response to Cephas does not mean, however, that he gives here a report of his remarks on the occasion of their confrontation. The Antioch incident *and* the Galatian situation shape his language and emphases. The passage moves from Antioch to Galatia, as it were, with no perceptible line of demarcation and thus serves as an effective bridge between the autobiographical accounts of 1:11–2:14 and the argument of 3:1–4:7.

Paul sustains the autobiographical note of the preceding accounts with the "I" of verses 18-21 while introducing terms and ideas that then quickly become the foci of his lengthy argument from scripture and experience. The particular issue at Antioch he generalizes by means of the category "works of the Law," a phrase that appears now for the first time. Likewise appearing for the first time in the letter are the verb *be justified* and the cognate noun *righteousness*, the verb *believe*, and the phrase "faith of [or in] Christ." Although it occurs only once (v. 21), the word *grace* picks up an important earlier emphasis (1:6, 15). This vocabulary leaves little doubt about what Paul considered the "truth" of the gospel that he had defended in Antioch and Jerusalem and that he is now defending again in Galatians.

"We ourselves," he writes, "Jews by birth and not 'sinners' of the Gentiles, knowing (or: because we know) that a human being is not justified by works of the Law, [knowing that a human being is not justified] except by means of Jesus-Christ-faith, we too (or: even we) believed on Christ Jesus so that we might be justified by Christ-faith and not by works of the Law—because by works of the Law all flesh will not be justified" (2:15-16 AT). This dense, compressed statement requires unpacking, piece by piece.

" 'Sinners' of the Gentiles" (NRSV: "Gentile sinners") reflects the standard Jewish conviction that non-Jews were, by definition, "sinners" because they lived outside the covenant with God, their conduct unrestrained by God's Law. By "works of the Law" Paul refers to those practices that Torah requires of that people which *is* bound to God by the Sinai covenant, practices that make the descendants of Abraham a *distinctive* people, set apart and holy, different from the nations (Gentiles). Works of the Law, then, function to identify God's covenant people. In Paul's phrase, "of the Law" actually has a double sense: works of the Law are those practices that Torah commands, yes; but at the same time they are practices that Torah *produces by* commanding, thereby ensuring the survival and distinctive identity of a people. In view of Gal 2:1-5, 11-14, we can assume that when Paul uses the expression in this letter, he has in mind, particularly, the requirement of circumcision and laws concerning food (what food was forbidden, how "clean" animals were to be slaughtered and prepared, possibly also such regulations as hand washing at meals).

English readers of Galatians need to be aware that the Greek words corresponding to *righteousness* and *justify* are formed on a common root, *dikai-*. We normally translate *dikaios* as "righteous" and *dikaiosynē* as "righteousness," but *dikaioun* as "to justify" and *dikaiousthai* as "to be justified." Thus, as we move from noun (or adjective) to verb (and vice versa), we are unsuspecting victims of a semantic shift completely foreign to the Greek. For Paul's Greek-speaking hearers, to be justified was to be regarded or acknowledged as righteous.

The verb *be justified* has its original home in the law court. In the Old Testament, one can be justified (acquitted, acknowledged to be right, judged righteous, granted a favorable verdict, vindicated) by God or by a human judge. In either case, the notion of relationship is always at least implicit. Thus persons are righteous if they fulfill the obligations fundamental to the particular relationship that pertains. Although one can, of course, make claims for oneself, whether a person has met the obligations of a relationship is, finally, the judgment of another. The "divine passive" of the verb that occurs four times in Gal 2:16-17 reflects this realization; the passive (e.g., "so that we might be justified") indicates that it is *God* who justifies.

When the psalmist says of God, "You are justified in your words" (Ps 51 [LXX 50]:4), he is acknowledging that God's judgment is right because he (the petitioner) is guilty. Often in the LXX, however, *dikaioun* has the sense of giving the *favorable* judgment that a person's behavior deserves (e.g., Deut 25:1; 2 Sam [LXX 2 Kgs] 15:4; 1 Kgs [LXX 3 Kgs] 8:32; Ps 73 [LXX 72]:13; Sir 23:11; 26:19, 31 [LXX 34]:5). More pertinent for our understanding of Galatians, though, is the affirmation that God will justify even though a person's (or a people's) conduct does *not* deserve a favorable verdict. In a psalm that Paul echoes at Gal 2:16, the psalmist pleads with God: "Do not enter into judgment with your servant, because all the living will not be justified in your sight (LXX Ps 142:2 [Heb 143:2]). Why no person can stand acceptable before God, the psalmist does not say. What is clear is that his hope for deliverance from his enemies rests not on his own worthiness but solely on God's steadfastness, righteousness, and mercy (vv. 1, 8, 11, 12). Here God is righteous, not because God gives the verdict warranted but because the deity saves one who can make no claim that he deserves a favorable judgment. The psalmist thus does not distinguish between God's righteousness and God's *mercy*.

In Sir 18:2 the sage declares that the Lord *alone* "will be justified" (AT); thus, by implication (and in agreement with the psalmist), no human being *will* be. He goes on to remark the brevity of human life and, in notable contrast to the power of God, the sobering limitations of human beings—limitations to which the deity responds by pouring mercy upon them (Sir 18:11), for "the mercy of the Lord is upon all flesh" (Sir 18:13 AT). In Micah 7 (LXX) the speaker, perhaps the nation itself, bewails the corruption of the people and the resulting punishment of God, but affirms, "I will look to the LORD, I will wait for the God of my salvation; my God will hear me" (v. 7). The speaker warns his enemy not to rejoice. He admits to having sinned but expresses confidence that God will rescue: "I shall suffer the wrath of the Lord because I sinned against him, until he justifies [i.e., judges favorably on] my case. And he will render my judgment and will bring me out into the light. I will see his righteousness" (v. 9).

Second Isaiah, too, recognizing the appropriateness of God's judgment upon the nation (43:22-24, 27-28), has the deity say, "Recall [your transgressions?] and let us contend with each other [i.e., in court]. First declare your lawless deeds so that you might be justified!" (v. 26 LXX). The divine sarcasm bears the truth that on the basis of her conduct Israel cannot possibly be vindicated. But in language that echoes Exod 3:14 the deity declares, "I am, I am the one who wipes out your transgressions, and I will by no means remember them" (43:25 LXX). In another word of comfort to a people in exile, Second Isaiah affirms, "All the seed of the sons of Israel will be justified by the Lord and in [or by] God will be glorified" (45:25 LXX). In Isaiah 50 the prophet (or perhaps the servant of the Lord, other than the prophet) does not share Israel's sin; but, insulted and abused like the people, he takes comfort in God's help: "I have set my face like solid rock, and I know that I will not be put to shame because the one who justifies me is near" (vv. 7-8a LXX).

Alongside such texts as these, a number of passages in the Thanksgiving Hymns from Qumran sound familiar. The psalmist often acknowledges that no human being is righteous before God (1QH 4.30-31; 7.16-17, 28-29; 9.14-16; 12.17, 32; 15.12; 16.11; also 1QS 11.9-10). Humans are able to "stand" only because of God's goodness, mercy, compassion, and grace (see 1QH 4.35-37; 7.18, 27, 30; 9.18-19, 33-34; 11.30-32; 13.16-17; 15.16; 16.16-17; also 1QS 11.12-15). It is God's Spirit that cleanses (16.12) and "makes perfect a way" for humans (4.31-32).

It is instructive to observe the kinds of nouns and verbs that the above texts associate so closely with God's justifying act: God is *savior;* God rescues, brings out into the light, wipes out transgressions, and glorifies; speakers affirm their confidence in God's steadfastness, God's goodness and righteousness, God's mercy and grace. A further observation is that none of these speakers makes a claim upon God. None says that he (or Israel or the elect) deserves God's favor. Indeed, several overtly confess their sinfulness, thereby acknowledging that God's vindication or acquittal contravenes human measures of rightness. The conviction that finds expression here is, apparently, that God overrides human standards and even the standards set forth in Torah because some wider purpose or some aspect of the divine nature is more fundamental than the need to balance wrongdoing with retributive justice. Nevertheless, nothing in these texts suggests that Torah is set aside or its requirements disregarded.

If we can take Paul at his word, the conviction that God does not justify persons because of works of the Law was not unique to his preaching or the Gentile mission. Even Cephas and, presumably, the Christian Jews of Antioch agreed (Gal 2:15-16). The biblical and post-biblical texts just examined allow us to glimpse one of the assumptions underlying this common conviction: The conduct of human beings, even those persons guided by Torah, is not deserving of the divine favor that is the essential source of human well-being. God "justifies"—vindicates or judges favorably—because of the goodness or righteousness or mercy that is constitutive of deity and remains, finally, mysterious.

In the Jesus-movement, the way of living in relationship with the God who justifies is *pistis.* Unfortunately, in English we must use one term, *faith,* to translate this noun, and another very different one, *believe,* to translate the cognate verb *pisteuein.* What Paul means by *faith* and *believe* we can discover from three lines of evidence: the connotations the words *pistis/pisteuein* would have carried in the first-century Mediterranean world; the meanings evident from Paul's use of these terms in other letters, which, we can assume, have some chance of reflecting the religious vocabulary he had used previously with the Galatians; and whatever clues the text of Galatians itself provides.

In view of the pervasive practice and study of rhetoric in the Greco-Roman world, it is highly probable that for Paul and his hearers *believe* would carry the connotation "be convinced or persuaded" and *faith* would bear the (subjective) sense "the personal state of being convinced" or the (objective) sense of a *conviction,* the consequence of being convinced (Kinneavy 1987). In the context of religious propaganda, verb and noun could name the experience of conversion: to believe was to accept as true the claims of a missionary preacher, to commit oneself to the deity proclaimed, and to become a part of the group that worshiped and served that deity. In the LXX, *pisteuein* (rendering the root *'mn* when a text is translated from Hebrew) can mean to accept some sign or utterance as true ("believe that," as at Exod 4:1, 5, 8, 9; perhaps Pss 27 [LXX 26]:13, 106 [LXX 105]:12; Sir 19:15; Isa 43:10; 53:1); to have confidence in (Deut 28:66; Sir 32:21, 24; Jer 12:6); to rely upon or trust in (e.g., Gen 15:6; Exod 14:31; Num 14:11; 20:12; Sir 11:21); or to obey (Deut 9:23; Jer 25:8). Sometimes *pisteuein* seems equivalent to fearing the Lord (Sir 2:8, 10) or hoping in God or God's salvation (Ps 78 [LXX 77]:22; Sir 2:6). At Isa 7:9; 28:16 the idea of trusting God seems indistinguishable from standing firm, and the noun *pistis,* too, can have the sense of faithfulness (in Deut 32:20 its antithesis is idolatry), constancy (Jer 15:18), or truthfulness (Jer 5:3; 7:28; 9:3). Often it is hardly possible to say which of these connotations is predominant, so easily do they cross and merge.

A number of these biblical dimensions of *pistis/pisteuein* are evident in Paul's letters. Romans 4 depicts *pistis* as the absolute entrustment of the self to God. In Rom 10:9-10, where confessing that Jesus is Lord parallels believing that God raised him from the dead, *pisteuein* obviously means to accept as true the Christian claim about Jesus, his death and resurrection (see also 1 Thess 4:14 and 1 Cor 15:11 in the context of vv. 3-8). Romans 1:5 makes explicit the *obedience* aspect of faith, and 14:23 requires that faith be understood as *conviction.* At 1 Cor 3:5, "servants [of God] through whom you came to believe" seems to mean "servants through whom you were converted"; and in the same letter (14:22) "believers" is Paul's matter-of-fact designation for committed members of the Christian community.

This brief excursion done, we return to Gal 2:15-16. Here Paul's antithesis "by faith and not by works of the Law" tells what faith is *not:* it is not a way of life that takes its direction from requirements of Torah such as being circumcised and avoiding certain foods. Positively, faith is a way determined by Christ. In twice affirming the means by which persons are justified, Paul uses the phrase *pistis (Iēsou) Christou* (which occurs also at Rom 3:22, 26 and Phil 3:9). What he means by this expression has been much debated in recent years, with some students of Paul's thought arguing for the translation "faith of Christ" and others insisting on "faith in Christ" (so NRSV).

Those who hold that Paul refers to faith *in* Christ (e.g., Betz 1979, 117; Hultgren 1980; Bruce 1982, 139; Fung 1988, 115; Dunn 1991) find the following points convincing. (1) At Gal 2:15 the apostle, in effect, defines *pistis* with the parallel verbal expression "believe in Christ." (2) Like "works of the Law," *pistis Christou* refers to the *human* element in the transaction of justification, the word *grace* referring to justification's divine source. (3) The Deutero-Pauline and Pastoral Epistles use the unambiguous phrase "faith in *[en]* Christ" (Eph 1:15; 1 Tim 1:13; 3:13, 15). The fact that Paul himself does *not*, suggests that he has his own expression that means the same thing—namely, *pistis Christou.* (4) Paul uses the verb "to believe" frequently with Christians (or Abraham) as its subject, but never with Christ as subject. If by *pistis Christou* he means Christ's own faith, how can one explain the fact that he never says that Christ *believed?*

Among the arguments marshaled by proponents of "faith(fulness) of Christ" (e.g., Johnson 1982; Hays 1983; Hooker 1989; Longenecker 1990, 87-88; Hays 1991; Matera 1992, 100-101), one finds the following: (1) Jesus' faith or faithfulness was clearly a tradition known in early Christianity (see Heb 2:17; 3:2; 12:2; Rev 1:5; 3:14; 19:11; possibly Jas 2:1), and Christ's obedience is an emphasis in Rom 5:15-19 and in the (likely) pre-Pauline hymn at Phil 2:5-11; (2) At Gal 3:23-25 Paul says that faith "came" and is "revealed." But how could faith *in* Christ, faith as a human act, "come" or be *revealed?* (3) If Paul wished to speak of faith *in* Christ, his failure to make his intention unambiguously clear by using a preposition (as in the Pastorals) is inexplicable, especially in light of the expressions "the faithfulness of God" (Rom 3:3) and "the faith of our father Abraham" (Rom 4:12 AT), expressions that would hardly predispose the recipients of Romans to understand *pistis Christou* as faith *in* Christ; (4) if *pistis Christou* means (human) faith in Christ, in several Pauline texts the phrase is redundant, for these texts also include some other expression designating human faith: "we have come to believe in Christ" (Gal 2:16); "those who believe" (Gal 3:22); "all who believe" (Rom 3:22); "through faith" (Phil 3:9). Responding to this observation, proponents of the "faith in Christ" view contend that in these texts *pistis Christou* is *emphatic,* not redundant. Their response fails to note, however, that no such "emphasis" marks other texts in which the word *faith* appears *without* the genitive *Christou!*

Galatians 2:16 and 3:22 share with two other *pistis Christou* texts three common features: (1) in each case, *pistis Christou* is part of a prepositional phrase ("by" or "through") indicating means; (2) each of these prepositional phrases expresses the means by which *God* rectifies the human situation; and (3) in each case, alongside the *pistis Christou* prepositional phrase we find another word or phrase referring unmistakably to *believers'* faith. These observations, taken together, suggest that *pistis Christou* names something *not* absolutely synonymous with the faith of believers—something, moreover, that is antecedent to, and (at least conceptually) distinguishable from, believers' faith, something that is the vehicle of God's rectifying act. God justifies or gives the Spirit *through* or *by pistis Christou to* those who believe. Especially revealing is the juxtaposition of Gal 3:14 and 3:22. In verse 22 *God gives* the Spirit by means of *pistis Christou;* in verse 14 *believers receive* the Spirit through *pistis.* It would appear, then, that God acts through the medium of Christ's faith on behalf of those persons who themselves have faith.

It is also the case, however, that Paul's usage does not consistently and cleanly differentiate between Christ's faith and the faith of believers. Note that at Rom 1:17 the righteousness of God is revealed [by God] "through faith for faith," whereas at Rom 3:21-22 the righteousness of God is manifested [by God] through *pistis Christou*. Similarly, Paul can say both that God justifies by *pistis* (Rom 3:28) and that God justifies through *pistis Christou* (Gal 2:16). Readers who find these observations compelling and who agree that Paul regarded Christ as a person of faith have two options. They can read "of Christ" as a genitive of possession or attribute (it designates Christ's own faith and nothing more) or they can construe the genitive in yet a different way.

In Greek, when it is used without preposition to indicate the relationship between two nouns, the genitive case can bear a variety of nuances. Quite obviously, in "the fruit of the Spirit" (Gal 5:22), the genitive functions differently than in "the gospel of Christ" (1:7); in "the right hand of fellowship" (2:9), than in "the grace of God" (2:21). The genitive can indicate apposition ("the promise of the Spirit" at 3:14 is the Spirit that was promised), place ("the churches of Galatia," 1:2), possession ("the womb of my mother," 1:15 AT), and relationship ("the brother of the Lord," 1:19). In general, one can say that the genitive *qualifies* the governing noun by somehow specifying its nature, character, class, or kind. I contend that in the phrase *pistis Christou* the genitive bears a sense different from either faith *in* Christ or faith *of* Christ. *Pistis Christou* is that faith which is characteristic of believers because they are "in Christ." It identifies those who are "in Christ" because it is, in its fundamental character, the same absolute trust and unwavering obedience that Jesus actualized and exemplified. It is that way of living in God's will that Christ *inaugurated* in the last days. Christ's own faith plays a decisive, indeed unique, role in the fulfillment of God's purpose for the world because it qualifies him as the single seed to whom God's promises were given and "in" whom all believers live (3:16, 26-28). Yet, in Galatians, Paul's emphasis falls not on Jesus' own believing/faithfulness (which, I will argue, *is* featured at 2:20) but on faith as it bears the character of Christ's own steadfastness, a steadfastness grounded in absolute confidence in, and reliance upon, God. Believers' faith, like his, is the way of death (2:19) and "new creation" (6:15). This faith, the very possibility and character of which derive from Christ's own, Paul calls *pistis Christou.* Thus Paul's phrase is a double-sided expression, referring first to the faith of Christ himself but including as well the answering faith of those who are in him (Williams 1987a).

An analogy may help to clarify my interpretation. In our society, *love* is a word with a wide range of meanings. If I wish to explain to someone that I am using this battered word to mean a self-giving devotion to others that does not flag even amidst unending need, love that endures although it can never "succeed," I might say, "You know, Mother Teresa-love!"—love *like* Mother Teresa's, yes, but more important, love that has become an existential possibility for many in our time because she actualized and exemplified this way of being human in our world.

According to the apostle, Christ-faith is believing "unto Christ." When Paul says, "We believed *eis Christon,*" most interpreters have understood him to be naming Christ as the "object" of faith: Christians "believe in Jesus." I contend that Paul's language in all his letters (and thus, presumably, in his missionary preaching as well) does not support this view. He never uses the expression "faith in Christ" *(pistis en Christō),* and insofar as one can speak of the "object" toward which faith is directed, for Paul that "object" is *God.* To appreciate what Paul means by "believe *eis Christon,*" we should give full weight to his use of the aorist rather than the present tense ("we believed," "we came to believe," rather than "we believe"). The aorist suggests a decisive moment of reorientation and commitment, and indeed that is just what Paul goes on to describe in verses 19-20. One way to render Paul's statement, then, is: "We have committed ourselves unto Christ." Another takes "Christ" as Pauline shorthand for "the gospel of what God is doing through Christ's death and resurrection." To "believe unto Christ" would thus be to accept as true the gospel whose "content" is the death and resurrection of Jesus Messiah. Alternatively, we can allow the preposition *eis* to retain its root sense of movement toward or into. In this case, to "believe into Christ" would be to move into that new socio-spiritual domain where Jesus Messiah is Lord and where his faith is source and pattern for those who are "in" him.

In the prepositional phrase "be justified *en Christō*" (2:17), *en* can have a locative or instrumental sense. If "*through* Christ,"

Christ is the means of justification by virtue of his death and resurrection; if "*in* Christ," Christ is the domain within which believers live in communion with the Risen One (contrast "in Judaism" at 1:13 and 1:14). If its locative sense dominates, Paul's phrase names believers' new social-spiritual "location," as "be justified" speaks of the new state and status of standing in God's favor. But *pistis/pisteuein* is not the cause or source of this state and location, and thus the familiar expression "justifying faith" is seriously misleading. Faith does not justify. *God* does—although "God" does not appear in Gal 2:15-17. The deity remains hidden in the passive form of the verb "be justified," perhaps because Paul wants the emphasis here to fall on the contrast between Christ-faith and works of the Law rather than on the one who justifies.

"We ourselves . . . we know" indicates that Paul thinks his fellow Christian Jews would agree with everything he says in 2:16. But if they did, how can we account for the disagreement between them and Paul regarding the "Gentile question"? If "works of the Law" were *not* the means by which anyone was justified, why did the Christian Jews of Antioch withdraw from table fellowship with Gentiles? Apparently Cephas and the rest did not consider their conviction (about the means of justification) and their action (withdrawal from table fellowship) to be incompatible. Gentiles and Jews were indeed justified by Christ-faith, but the "people from James" had persuaded them that Christian Jews should nevertheless continue to observe those laws of Torah whose practice safeguarded the distinctive identity of Abraham's descendants. Paul cannot agree. From a shared conviction he draws a very different conclusion: Works of the Law are superfluous and should therefore not be allowed to separate Gentiles and Jews. The ethnic identity of Christian Jews and Christian Gentiles could not both be sustained. The issue of table fellowship made it clear that one or the other had to give way. Either, in effect, Gentiles had to become Jews or Jews had to become Gentiles. Paul sees no other alternative, and for him the right course was clear: Jews had to become as Gentiles.

The reasoning behind Paul's conclusion does not become clear immediately. First he tries to deflect a possible accusation (or, perhaps, a real one): anyone who dispenses with works of the Law for us Christian Jews becomes a "sinner" and thereby makes Christ, in effect, sin's servant. In the if-clause of verse 17 Paul acknowledges that he and others were indeed found to be sinners. That is, it had become obvious that they were living in a way prohibited by Torah and thus no different from Gentiles (recall "Gentile sinners" in v. 15). One might expect the apostle further to acknowledge boldly that since this Law-free way of life implicated Christ, Christ was indeed a "servant of sin." Instead he exclaims "Certainly not!" But why does the expected conclusion not follow? Clearly Christ *is* a "servant of sin" if sin is what Torah says it is. This, however, is precisely the point that Paul will not grant. Yes, he is saying, we who advocate dispensing with works of the Law are indeed "sinners" according to Torah, but we do not thereby make Christ a servant of sin. Why? Because Torah is no longer the definer and arbiter of sin. Christ is not a servant of sin because "sin" is not what Torah says it is, at least not insofar as relations between Christian Jews and Christian Gentiles are concerned.

The particle *gar* ("for," "indeed," "in fact") at the beginning of verse 18 (NRSV: "but") tells us that this verse follows upon, and is connected directly to, the point of verse 17, particularly Paul's sharp denial of the idea that Christ is a servant of sin. The nature of the connection, however, is by no means clear. Indeed, a gap appears between the two verses. The bridge between them, I propose, is a thought left unspoken that amounts to this: Christ is certainly *not* a servant of sin; one can so regard him only if the Law remains the definer and arbiter of sin, and that is exactly what I [Paul] refuse to do. "Indeed *(gar)*, if I build back what I tore down, I prove myself a transgressor" (AT). This statement has given interpreters no little trouble. Is Paul *admitting* or *denying* that he is "building back"? What *is* it that he admits or denies building back? Does "prove myself a transgressor" mean a transgressor *then* or a transgressor *now*, a transgressor in tearing down or in building back? Does "transgressor" mean one who has contravened the will or God or one who has dispensed with the laws of Torah? In addressing such questions, the task is to hear verse 18 as a connecting link between verse 17 and verse 19.

Paul's shift from "we" (vv. 15-17) to "I" (v. 18) indicates that he is no longer speaking about what he and Cephas hold in common. In verses 18-20 he certainly speaks about himself, but his "I" is inclusive. The "I" of these verses is what might be called the "hortative I." That is, Paul is implicitly urging his hearers to follow his example, the example of a man who lives out the truth of the gospel. Two terms provide the key to what he is recommending or condemning: *tear down* and *transgressor.* One can hear the first, *katalyein,* as a synonym of "destroy" *(porthein)* at 1:13, 23 and can observe that Paul elsewhere uses its antonym "build up" with reference to the churches (Rom 15:20; 1 Cor 14:4, 5, 12, 17, 26; 2 Cor 10:8; 12:19; 13:10; 1 Thess 5:11). Thus Paul might be saying: By now building back the church that I was once destroying, I prove that I was *then* a transgressor against God. Or he might be saying instead: By building back the church, I prove myself a transgressor *now* against the Law. The implicit warning would be either "Do not transgress as I did, do not destroy the church by insisting on works of the Law." Or it would be "Do not hesitate to 'transgress' as I do, for the Law no longer defines sin."

Attractive as it is, the view that the object of "tear down" is the *church* suffers from two weaknesses. First, unless "build back" was part of Paul's missionizing vocabulary (which is unlikely), the Galatians would not know how he elsewhere used the word. Second, *katalyein* is not really a very close synonym of *porthein. Porthein* is a political/military term meaning to besiege, ravage, plunder, ruin, or destroy. *Katalyein* means to dissolve, dismantle, abolish, bring to an end, make invalid, or destroy. Had Paul wished to refer to destroying the *church,* he could have made his intent much clearer had he used the same verb we find at 1:13, 23.

In light of the issues of table fellowship at Antioch and circumcision in the Galatian churches, Paul's metaphors of tearing down (dismantling, abolishing) and building back would seem to refer most naturally to the laws of Torah that identify Jews as a distinctive people and keep them separate from Gentile "sinners." We should not simply assume, however, that *parabatēs* ("transgressor") here means one who transgresses the Law. The nouns *transgressor* and *transgression* are related (by common root) to the verb *parabainein.*

This verb can mean "to overstep, transgress," but in the LXX it also has the sense "to turn aside or deviate from" (LXX Exod 32:8; Deut 9:12, 16; 11:16; 17:20; 28:14; Josh 11:15; 1 Kgs [Heb 1 Sam] 12:21; Dan 9:5; see also Sir 23:18; 42:10; Acts 1:25). The notion of deviating from is, of course, ready at hand in this passage, for just three sentences earlier Paul had recounted that at Antioch, Cephas and Barnabas and the other Christian Jews were not "walking straight" with respect to (or toward) the truth of the gospel. The Galatians, then, might well have heard Paul saying: If I build back the laws that I tore down (laws that keep Gentiles and Jews separate), I thereby show myself to be a "deviator" from the truth of the gospel—and I am no deviator.

Paul does not aver merely that he refuses to build back the Law. "In fact," he continues in verse 19, "I [the pronoun is emphatic] through the Law to the Law died so that to God I might live" (AT). In the Greek no prepositions clarify the dative case of the second "the Law" or "God," but the dative is the case used to indicate the *relation* of a person to something. To die is to sever relation. To die (with reference) to the Law is to sever the bond between the Law and self that heretofore had determined one's perspective and direction. It is also to obviate the Law's power to judge and condemn. This dying to the Law is necessary if one is to "live to God" (*why*, the apostle does not explain), but what Paul means by dying by *means of* the Law is not clear. He may allude to a conclusion he could have come to earlier, that since Deut 21:23 curses God's Messiah, Torah cannot be infallible. "Through the Law" may allude to the new reading of Torah that his conversion-call compelled him to undertake, a reading that revealed a divine purpose that disallowed the Law's own ethnocentric prescriptions. But his wording "through the Law to the Law" (*dia nomou nomō*) may owe as much to its aural effect as to any profound insight or any claim that the Law was itself the cause of its loss of power.

This death to the Law Paul further describes as being crucified with Christ. Christ's crucifixion was preliminary to his resurrection, and the Risen One lives a life different in its manner and mode than the life of the one who was crucified. Correspondingly, Paul's dying to the Law means that the "I," the *egō*, that he was is no more. The emphasis on *identifying* with Christ, obvious already in the phrase "Christ-faith" and in the clause "I have been crucified with Christ," appears again in the second clause of verse 20: "Christ lives *en emoi.*" This clause is not be be limited to some private, mystical experience. *En emoi,* the same phrase Paul used at 1:16 and 1:24, means "in my life": Christ is manifest in the whole range of personal decisions and relationships and commitments. This life—Paul calls it "what I now live in the flesh" (AT), that is, life in this present age, subject to all the weaknesses and failings and disappointments that afflict humanity—he says he lives "in faith." Once again the preposition *en* can bear an instrumental as well as a locative sense: faith is the means by which one lives before God, but faith also determines the shape and boundaries of life. Instead of using the phrase "Christ-faith," as in 2:16, Paul here defines faith with a clause. His sentence reads: "in faith I live—that [faith] of the son of God who loved me and gave himself up for me" (2:20 AT). The that-clause defines the faith in and by which Paul lives *as* the faith of God's son, that faith characteristic of the son and manifested in his love and self-giving. Just as in verse 20*ab* Christ is the real subject acting in and through Paul's life, so in verse 20*c* the faith of the son of God is the distinctive character of his new "I." Because Christ now lives "in me," Christ's exemplary faith has become Paul's own mode of personal existence before God, that mode of existence that earlier Paul called "Christ-faith."

In verse 21 we can, finally, glimpse the logic prompting Paul to insist that *because* persons stand in God's favor by means of Christ-faith, works of the Law cannot be allowed to separate Gentiles from Jews and thus Christian Jews must become as Gentiles: to allow the Law to define sin and arbitrate the relation of Jews and Gentiles in the church would be to nullify the grace of God (v. 21*a*). One recalls that God had called Paul to apostleship "through his grace" (1:15) and had called the Galatians "in the grace of Christ" (1:6). For Paul to "nullify" the grace of God, then, would be tantamount to denying that the Gentiles stood justified before God. To nullify God's grace would be to scrap the gospel he preached and admit that his life work as a slave of Christ was a huge mistake. This he cannot do. The Galatians may desert the One who called them in grace, but Paul will not.

A Note on Galatians and Acts: In the modern history of New Testament scholarship a much discussed issue has been how to reconcile Gal 1–2 with Acts 9–15—or whether even to try (Knox 1954, 61-73; Caird 1962, 605-7; Jewett 1979, 63-93). Can Paul's account of his conversion and his postconversion activity be made to fit Acts 9:1-30? Is Peter's withdrawal from table fellowship with Gentiles in Antioch (according to Paul's account) fully compatible with Acts 10:1-11, 18? Does the Jerusalem conference of Gal 2 correspond to the council of Acts 15? If so, how does one reconcile the private nature of one (Gal 2:2) with the public character of the other (Acts 15:4-6, 22), and how does one account for the disagreement at Antioch in light of the council decision set forth at Acts 15:19? The effort to avoid such questions by identifying the visit of Gal 2:1-10 with that of Acts 11:27-30 or 18:22-23 instead of Acts 15 raises new and equally difficult problems.

In attempting to reconcile Gal 1–2 with Acts, scholars have almost invariably taken Paul's account at face value while regarding Luke's as tendentious. Caution, though, is in order here. As one student of the New Testament writes: "The influence of the ancient rhetorical tradition made moral persuasion a higher value than historical truth. Ancient autobiographies were more concerned with ethical characterization and edification than with chronology and exactitude" (Lyons 1985, 60). In Galatians, Paul seeks to persuade, and in 1:6–2:21 his discourse is hardly disinterested, his characterization of others hardly unbiased. What he includes and what he omits, what he chooses to emphasize and how he goes about saying it, all serve his primary end. The resulting document is an invaluable historical source, but only when read as cautiously and as critically as any other.

◊ ◊ ◊ ◊

One indicator of Paul's purpose in Gal 1:6–2:21 is a concentration of three particular terms: "I," "(proclaim the) gospel," and "Gentiles." The first-person singular pronoun or verb ending occurs here some sixty-five times, and then its frequency drops off sharply. "Gospel" and "proclaim the gospel" (*euangelion* and *euangelizesthai*) occur twelve times in this section (noun: 1:6, 7, 11; 2:2, 5, 7, 14; verb: 1:8, 9, 11, 16, 23), twice in the phrase "the truth of the gospel" (2:5, 14), then two times later in the letter (4:13, and "proclaim the gospel beforehand" at 3:8). "Gentiles" *(ethnē)* appears seven times here (1:16; 2:2, 8, 9, 12, 14, 15), then again at 3:8, 14. These lines cross, as it were, to reveal one of Paul's principal aims in this letter: to present himself as the uncompromising defender of the truth of the gospel for the Gentiles. This self-presentation lays the foundation for everything that follows. Drawing upon past experiences particularly relevant to the issues facing the Galatian churches, he establishes his character and credibility. According to the categories of the rhetorical handbooks, he is fashioning an "ethical" proof, *ethos* meaning one's distinctive moral character. Implicitly, he is at the same time saying to the Galatians, "*You* can do—and be—no less."

In commending a particular stance by means of his own example, the apostle leaves no room for maneuver and compromise. Sharp antitheses course throughout this section: another (different) gospel and God (1:6); a "human sort" of gospel and the gospel received through revelation (1:11-12); Paul's former life "in Judaism" and his life as proclaimer of the good news to the Gentiles (1:13-14 and 1:18–2:14); freedom and enslavement (2:4); "false brothers" and Paul as defender of the truth of the gospel (2:4-5); Cephas's "hypocrisy" and (by implication) Paul's "walking straight" in accord with the truth of the gospel (2:13-14); justification by works of the Law and justification by Christ-faith (2:16); building up and tearing down (2:18); living to God and living to the Law (the implied opposite of dying to the Law: 2:19); and righteousness through the Law and (by implication) righteousness from the grace of God (2:21). The conviction underlying all these antitheses derives ultimately from the great life reversal that Paul alludes to at 2:15-16. His transformative experience, then, is the principal source of the either/or perspective so obvious in the antitheses of Gal 1–2. One thing Paul's pairs of opposites show is that he does not honor the views of others, like Cephas or the "false brothers," who draw different behavorial imperatives from their common convictions as Jesus-people. He is no champion of one of the dominant virtues of our age: tolerance. But no matter how admirable one might regard his steadfastness, his attitude raises several provocative questions. First, how can religious persons, particularly those who testify to some undeniably real life-changing experience, avoid certain divisive effects of their own *certainty?* Can personal commitment coexist with openness to, and tolerance for, those whose certainties differ? What prevents uncompromising commitment from becoming an arrogant demand that others conform? And what keeps firm conviction from transmuting into fanaticism? Galatians 1–2 raises the questions but provides no answers.

The "autobiographical" section of Galatians also raises questions for Christians about the nature and limits of biblical authority. Although no one can show that they *did,* the "false brothers" at the Jerusalem conference and the "people from James" at Antioch certainly could have appealed to scriptural texts like Gen 17:9-14 to support their more "conservative" position. According to that text, by God's own command "every male among you" is to be circumcised, whether native-born Israelite or foreigner. The wording of Gen 17:13 is definitive and unyielding: "and my covenant shall be upon your flesh an eternal covenant" (LXX); the uncircumcised male "has broken my covenant" (v. 14). Why does such language not deter Paul from setting circumcision aside as a requirement for Gentile converts? Surely not because of what he learned from his reading of Scripture during his life "in Judaism" (Gal 1:14). As Gal 3 will demonstrate several times over, Paul *uses* Scripture to support his stance as a radical Christian Jew, but that stance does not *originate* in his reading of the Scriptures. The testimony of Gal 1 and 2 is that it originates in a personal revelation that then supplies the perspective from which Paul reads with different eyes. To be sure, the apostle seems convinced that only now does he really see what was "there" all along. Nevertheless, readers of Galatians cannot fail to realize that it was "a revelation of Jesus Christ" (1:12), *not* his reading of Scripture, that remade him into a slave of Christ. Tantalizingly brief though it is, his testimony in Gal. 1 sets the authority of his personal conversion experience in some tension with the authority later claimed for infallible Church or infallible Book.

Because of their reverence for the Bible as the "word of God," Christian readers of Galatians have naturally assumed that, in his disagreement with the agitators, Paul has not only the *better* argument but that his is the *only* position worthy even of being taken seriously. His "opponents" in Jerusalem, Antioch, and Galatia, it has seemed apparent to many, rejected his gospel of justification by grace because they were narrow-minded "legalists" who believed that humans could achieve God's favor by their good works.

But Christians do not honor Paul, or the Bible that includes his letters, if they so caricature those fellow believers with whom he vigorously disagreed. We can fully appreciate the apostle only if we acknowledge the sensibleness of his antagonists' views and the validity of their concerns. Not without reason did they regard Paul as a dangerous radical who threatened to surrender the most precious distinctives of that people whom the one true God had called out from among the nations to bear witness to God's truth in all the earth. We have no letter from *their* pen, but Paul's adversaries could have argued their case by claiming to be defenders of God's word! It was *God,* not they, who commanded all Israel not to eat certain foods. It was *God's* will that Israel be a priestly kingdom and a holy nation (Exod 19:6), her distinctiveness safeguarded precisely by keeping God's commandments. Throughout the Mediterranean world, Jews regarded the Law as a divine gift, the supreme guide in the human quest to master harmful passions and desires. Indeed, it was the Law's reputation for superior instruction in self-mastery that made Judaism attractive to many Gentiles. Even more important, perhaps, for many first-century Jews was the Law's function as the paramount safeguard against idolatry—prohibited by the first of the Ten Commandments and regarded by Jews as the severest threat to peoplehood and holiness. According to the *Epistle of Aristeas* (second century BCE?), "the legislator," Moses, "surrounded us with unbroken palisades and iron walls to prevent our mixing with any of the other peoples in any matter, being thus kept pure in body and soul, preserved from false beliefs, and worshiping the only God omnipotent over all creation" (139; Charlesworth 1985, 22). But Moses' prohibitions regarding food and drink and clothes were not an end in themselves. Indeed, "such concerns are of no account among the people of our race, but throughout the whole of their lives their main objective is concerned with the sovereignty of God. So, to prevent our being perverted by contact with others or by mixing with bad influences, he hedged us in on all sides with strict observances connected with meat and drink and touch and hearing and sight, after the manner of the Law" (141-42). Without this "hedge" of the Law's strict observances, Israel could not fulfill her vocation—indeed, could not *be* the people of God!

Paul tells us that at Jerusalem and at Antioch he had resisted the efforts of others to make Gentile Jesus-converts into Jews. Was it the case, then, that these Gentiles did not belong to the people of God? By no means. Rather, Paul has reconceived God's people. One of the main assumptions that seems to underlie the position he describes himself taking at Jerusalem and Antioch is that in the last days God is abolishing religio-cultural barriers between peoples, and between people, and is creating a universal human family open to all who recognize and respond (faith!) to what God is about. It would appear that at Jerusalem and again at Antioch and now as he writes this letter, the apostle was preoccupied with the oneness of the new people of God. He championed a certain egalitarianism among persons of all ethnic and social backgrounds, an egalitarianism grounded in nothing less than the impartiality of the One who had called him in grace. One of the ironies of Galatians, though, is that Paul issues an order to *exclude* (the *anathema* of 1:8-9) on behalf of the inclusiveness of the end-time people of God! Must it ever be so? Does the yearning for an inclusive human community inevitably drive visionaries to exclude those who challenge their convictions about the conditions of inclusiveness? Does the desire to actualize our common humanity in and through our religious and cultural institutions invariably shun difference and confuse sameness with God's peace?

Attentive readers of Galatians will be aware of the diverse and frequent metaphors that Paul employs to press his case. His reliance on metaphor is hardly surprising, for metaphors structure how humans perceive and conceptualize our world (Lakoff and Johnson 1980, 3-4), and, as a son of Israel, Paul was steeped in scriptures rich in trope and image. In Gal 1:6–2:21 a series of movement metaphors illuminates his view of human life devoted to God. When he was living "in Judaism," he says he *advanced* in religious zeal beyond many of his contemporaries (1:14). He accuses the Galatians of *turning away* from (NRSV: "deserting") the One who called them (1:6). As slave of Christ and apostle to the Gentiles, he has *run* (2:2). Barnabas was "*carried* [or swept] *away*" (NRSV: "led astray") by the views of the other Christian Jews of Antioch (2:13), and Paul charges him and all the rest with not *walking straight* (NRSV: "acting consistently") in accord with (or toward) the truth of the gospel (2:14). These metaphors, reminiscent of the widely used scriptural figure of walking in the way of the Lord, suggest that Paul envisioned life before God as being "on the way" to a state or condition different from what prevails at present. To be called by God (1:6, 15) is not to be miraculously transported to the destination. The way requires direction (that is, proper orientation), effort, and steadiness.

To bring to language the personal experience that transformed persecutor into apostle, Paul turns to a less expected metaphor: death. Like any trope, this one too can be overpressed. When he says (and, recall, the "I" may be not merely personal) "I have been crucified with Christ" (2:19), he does not deny a continuity between I-past and I-present, a continuity rooted in memory (1:13-14). He still speaks Greek, not Coptic or Syriac. His sensibilities and symbolic world are still those of a first-century Jew. And yet, he testifies, he is not the person he used to be. His experience has so reordered the self he was that his previous self seems no longer there. We glimpse his sense of being no longer there and no longer in charge in the odd grammatical subject of verse 20*c*: not the pronoun "I," but rather "[what] I now live in the flesh"—as though this "what" is not himself at all. Indeed his "I-but-no-longer-I" speaks his awareness that the agential presence now operative is not his own self but the self of Christ crucified and raised by the power of God: "Christ . . . lives in me" (v. 20*b*). Here (vv. 19-20), as so often elsewhere, Paul is at least as much poet as theologian as he searches for language and reaches for images appropriate to his experience of Christ. To regard such affirmations as dogmatic propositions rather than as evocative metaphors is to become preoccupied with notes upon a page but fail to hear the music.

The Evidence of the Spirit (3:1–4:11)

In Gal 3:1 Paul turns from recounting evidence of his steadfast allegiance to the gospel and addresses the Galatians directly (3:1-5). But the second-person pronoun soon disappears, replaced by the third person ("they," "all," everyone," "no one") and the inclusive Christian "we," which predominate until the plural "you" reappears late in this section (3:26, 27, 28, 29; 4:6; singular: 4:7).

Traditionally regarded as the theological center of the letter, this section, as rhetoric, constitutes Paul's principal "logical proof," an attempt to persuade by emphasizing ideas and appealing to the experience and reason of his hearers. The argument does not divide neatly into "the evidence of experience" (3:1-5) and "the evidence of scripture" (what follows), as a quick first reading might suggest. Throughout the whole section, sometimes quite allusively, Paul continues to connect his argument with the Galatians' experience of the Spirit (3:14, 18, 21, 29; 4:6-7). Indeed, readers of the letter can profitably regard 3:6–4:7 as Paul's effort to convince the Galatians that they can confidently rely on their experience of the Spirit as proof of their new status as "heirs" because that experience is fully consonant with the divine plan revealed in Scripture. The Spirit received by faith (3:2, 5) gives proof of sonship by its Abba-cry (4:6-7). At its end, then, Paul's argument returns to its point of beginning, the experience of the Spirit thus framing all that intervenes.

Galatians 4:8-11 functions as a transition passage between the argument of 3:2–4:7 and the personal appeal of 4:12-20. Its rhetorical question (v. 9) and charge (v. 10) correspond to the rebuke and question of 3:1 and express the same exasperation.

The Experience of the Spirit and the Testimony of Scripture (3:1-14)

At 3:1 Paul addresses the Galatians not as "brothers" (cf. 1:11) but as "Galatians." His adjective *anoētos* might bear more than its basic sense "foolish, mindless, lacking intelligence"; it might also allude stingingly to the ethnic Galatians' ancient reputation as uneducated and barbaric. In his question "Who has cast a spell on you?" (AT), Paul uses a verb *(baskanein)* that, in the classical Mediterranean world, means to harm someone through the "evil eye." We need not understand Paul's language literally as an accusation of witchcraft, though. It is rather a suggestive metaphor underscoring how inexplicable, unreasonable, and deleterious is their yielding to the preachments of the agitators. (Note the use of witchcraft language, roots *baskan-* and *[kata]goēt-* in Plato *Republic* 413e; Philo *Spec. Leg.* 1.9; Wis 4:12.) In Greek, 3:1 is all one sentence: "O mindless Galatians, who has cast a spell on you, to whom virtually before your eyes Jesus Christ was publicly presented [as] crucified?" (AT). The phrase *kat' ophthalmous,* literally "according to the eyes," has the force of an adverb; in conjunction with the verb "to set forth in a public pronouncement" it reminds the Galatians of the vividness with which Paul had initially presented the Crucified One. Since Jesus' redemptive death was the event that opened the way for Gentiles to enter the end-time people of God, Paul finds incomprehensible the Galatians' apparent determination to make that death of no moment by seeking God's favor through the Law.

"The only thing I want to learn from you" (3:2) is a transparent rhetorical ploy. Paul needs to learn nothing from the Galatians. He knows very well how they must answer the questions that follow. His purpose is to force them to confront the most undeniable feature of their personal history as believers. This he will not let them forget, and its full implication he will not let them deny. What he wants "to learn" he asks in two questions. The first is, "Did you receive the Spirit by doing the works of the Law or by *akoēs pisteōs?*" The Greek phrase is subject to different translations, primarily because *akoē* can mean either the act (or faculty) of hearing or *what* is heard (thus a message or report). Paul's phrase could, therefore, mean "the message of faith," the proclamation that features faith. Another possibility, preferred here, is "the hearing of faith," that "hearing" called "faith." In the Old Testament, *hearing* is the preeminent mode of apprehending God. To *hear* the word of the

Lord is to *heed,* to respond appropriately to a command or threat or promise. Paul's phrase, then, is richly suggestive: faith is like hearing; indeed, faith is a kind of hearing/heeding. Like hearing, faith is "passive," the receiving of a word that comes from elsewhere, outside the self; but, like hearing, faith is also active, impossible without alert appropriation. Paul's apt metaphor nicely captures the receptivity and responsiveness of faith. It also suggests something of faith's mystery. Hearing is a phenomenon that we often take part in without prior intent to do so, because sound can assault us suddenly and from all sides; there is no auditory equivalent of averting one's eyes. Thus, an announcement of disaster or great good fortune, for example, or a threat or plea or promise can sometimes catch a person up and, it seems, effect its own response, a response of the self riveted and engaged. In such instances, hearing seems to be something that *happens to* us at least as much as it is something that we decide to do. And so it is with faith. Who can force herself to believe? Who can will himself to have faith? Faith is the engaged response, the yielding of the self, to an enthralling, captivating word, the gospel of Christ crucified and raised. Indeed, faith is the state of *being* captivated, but in a way that involves all one's faculties (Williams 1989).

This hearing that is faith is the means by which persons "receive" the Spirit. The unavoidable answer to the question of verse 2 Paul does not state, but he knows that as the letter is read to them the Galatians can respond in only one way. It is their earlier experience of the Spirit that makes their present behavior so incomprehensible. "Are you so foolish?" he queries. "Having started with the Spirit, are you now ending with the flesh?" (v. 3). "Flesh"—the limited, the weak, the merely human—stands in provocative contrast to "Spirit," the more so when we catch the pointed allusion to the rite of circumcision, the sign of God's covenant "in your flesh" (Gen 17:13). Since "end, finish" can also bear the connotation of being made perfect, Paul could be alluding to the agitators' claim that circumcision brings to completion the religious journey that began with hearing the gospel and experiencing the Spirit. But the notion that receiving the Spirit had to be supplemented by anything at all was utter nonsense for Paul. The outpouring of the Spirit upon

Gentiles was proof both dramatic and sufficient that God was incorporating them into the deity's end-time people (see Joel 2:28-29, quoted in the Pentecost story of Acts 2; also 1QS 4.18-21). To consider taking upon themselves the obligations of Torah in spite of such palpable evidence of God's election was to forfeit their call in grace (see 1:6). Thus, Paul inquires: "Did you experience so much for nothing?—if it really was for nothing" (v. 4). Just under the surface of this allusive appeal not to forfeit what had been given them lies the idea that their ultimate well-being is decidedly at stake. The word here translated "experience" also, in some contexts, means to *suffer.* If the Galatians had, in fact, suffered harassment or social dislocation because of their conversion, they could have heard this connotation in 3:4. The immediate context, though, both fore and aft (vv. 2, 5), allows them to hear the verb as a reference to their experience of the Spirit.

The question of verse 2 Paul reiterates in verse 5, although with different emphasis: God as giver of the Spirit and source of miraculous deeds. Again Paul anticipates the unavoidable response, and it is that silent response ("It is by faith-hearing that God bestows the Spirit and works miracles among us" [AT]) that provides the connection between verse 5 and verses 6-7 (a connection that the NRSV conceals by beginning a new paragraph with v. 6). "Just as [that is, in the same way as your faith-hearing] Abraham 'believed God, and it was reckoned to him as righteousness,' " the apostle continues, quoting Gen 15:6. "Understand [or you know], then, that 'faith people,' *they* are Abraham's sons!" [AT]. The word here translated "just as" does not normally begin a sentence unless it is followed by "so also," and some interpreters take it as an abbreviation for the standard formula "as it is written" by which Paul introduces quotations from Scripture (Betz 1979, 137). The root meaning of the word, though, is *correspondence,* and in the LXX it is often best rendered "in the same way." That translation here permits us to discern the correspondence between Abraham and Jesus-people that Paul is highlighting.

The correspondence between Abraham and Christians rests on three points of similarity. First, the Galatians' "hearing of faith" ("faith" = *pistis*) mirrors Abraham's believing/trusting God (the verb is *pisteuein*). Second, in both cases, believing/trust was the fitting human response to a word that comes from God. Abraham trusted/believed God when the deity promised him that his descendants would be as numerous as the stars of heaven (Gen 15:5); the Galatians believed the gospel of Christ crucified (see Gal 3:1). Third, for both Abraham and the Galatians, faith was the personal response essential for the eventual blessing that the divine word had initiated: God regarded Abraham's faith as "righteousness," that state necessary for divine favor and right relation with human beings; upon the Galatians God poured out the divine Spirit and worked miracles among them. "Receive the Spirit" in Galatians, sounds quite different, of course, from " reckoned . . . as righteousness" in Genesis, and the correspondence Paul is stressing would be neater if he had quoted a scripture affirming that Abraham received the Spirit. That he could not do, though, for the very good reason that Scripture includes no such statement. For Paul, though, the present experience of the Spirit bears witness to a right relationship with God; because of the "miraculous deeds" that God effects through it, the Spirit is, as it were, open to public viewing in a way that "righteousness" cannot be. Paul cannot conceive of the one apart from the other: receiving the Spirit and being reckoned righteous imply each other (Williams 1987b).

Two features of verse 7 attract attention. Instead of saying, "You know, then, that 'faith people' are sons of Abraham," we find an emphatic "they": "You know, then, that 'faith people,' *they* are Abraham's sons" (AT). And "then" (or "therefore") indicates that Paul is basing this contention upon the Genesis text quoted. One notes, however, that neither his quotation nor anything in its Genesis context claims that Abraham's descendants are "faith people." The apostle thus appears to be positing an answer to the question, "Who are the real descendants of Abraham?" It is likely that such a question is important to him (and to the Galatians) because the agitators have identified Abraham's true descendants as those persons who, like him and all members of his household, are circumcised (Gen 17). Abraham was, after all, the first human being to abandon idolatry and obey God's Law (see *Jub.* 11.16-17; 12.2-8, 16-24; *Bib. Ant.* 6.4; 23.5; *Apoc. Abr.* 1–8, 27.7, 31.4-8;

Philo *Virt.* 212-16; and Philo *Abr.* 3–6; Josephus *Ant.* 1 §154-57). He was thus a perfect exemplar the agitators could present for emulation. For his part, Paul contends that what makes persons children of Abraham is not circumcision but *faith:* as Abraham had faith, so do his true descendants.

My expression "faith people" translates Paul's phrase *hoi ek pisteōs,* the article *the* plus the preposition *from* (or *by*) plus the noun *faith.* The phrase has both a personal and a sociological reference: those persons whose lives are characterized by *pistis* and who, consequently, belong to a distinctive social grouping, the community of persons shaped by that same conviction-trust-commitment. Functioning as the name of a class of people ("Christians" in the language of the later Jesus-movement), "the [ones] of faith" is equivalent to "believers/those who believe" at 3:22 and corresponds to "the [ones] of circumcision" (AT) at 2:12. Because of the earlier conjunction of the phrase "by faith" with receiving the Spirit (3:2) and being justified (2:16), *hoi ek pisteōs* can be regarded as Pauline shorthand for "those who by faith are justified (reckoned righteous) and receive the Spirit."

At Gal 3:8 Scripture makes its appearance as an actor-agent in the grand story of God's dealings with humankind. In effect a surrogate for the deity, Scripture "foresaw" what God would do in the last days and "proclaimed [NRSV: declared] the gospel beforehand" (a single verb in Greek) to Abraham. The gospel that Abraham heard, Paul finds in Gen 12:3 ("all the tribes of the earth will be blessed in you" LXX) and 18:18 ("all the nations/Gentiles of the earth will be blessed in him" LXX). Significantly, the import of the "gospel" that Paul discerns in these conflated texts is ecclesial rather than christological. The gospel proclaimed beforehand to Abraham announces the inclusion of all peoples in the people of God.

Following Paul's argument requires close attention to the logic of verse 8. Scripture proclaimed to Abraham the gospel that "all the Gentiles shall be blessed in you" *because* Scripture foresaw that God would justify the Gentiles by faith. For the Genesis quotation to correspond exactly with what Scripture foresaw of God's future plan, one must conclude that "will be blessed" means that *God* will

bless and that God *blesses* the Gentiles by *justifying* them. Furthermore, to be blessed "in you [Abraham]" is to be blessed *as* Abraham's sons (v. 7); since persons are sons of Abraham "by faith," to
be "blessed in you" is to be justified by faith. The correspondence
between Abraham and Christians becomes even clearer when one
realizes that God's reckoning faith *(pisteuein)* as righteousness
(dikaiosynē), the language of Gen 15:6, is exactly equivalent to
God's justifying *(dikaioun)* by faith *(pistis).* Were he to rephrase
Gen 15:6 in his own language, Paul would say, "Abraham be-
lieved/trusted God, and he was justified by his faith."

Verse 9 clinches the Abraham/Christian parallel: "The upshot
[that is, what follows from vv. 5-8] is that faith people are blessed
along with the trusting/believing *[pistos]* Abraham" (AT), just as
Scripture foresaw (Gen 12:3/18:8); and they are blessed just as
Abraham was, by being reckoned righteous.

The obvious counterparts "by faith"/"by works of [the] Law"
and "blessed"/"under a curse" tempt the reader to regard verses 9
and 10*a* as exact antitheses: those of faith are blessed along with
Abraham, but those of works of the Law are under a curse. A closer
look, however, requires that this first impression be modified. The
term that connects verse 10 with what precedes is not the adversa-
tive conjunction *alla* or *de* ("but"). It is, rather, the conjunction *gar*
("for," "indeed"). Some thought seems to be missing between 9 and
10, something like, "The same cannot be said for those of the Law.
Indeed. . . . "

The exact relation of verse 10 to verse 9 has not occupied
interpreters nearly as much as has the connection between the two
parts of verse 10—the quotation from Deut 27:26 and the assertion
that Paul uses this quotation to substantiate. Discerning that connection is complicated by an apparent discrepancy: the quotation
features a curse upon all who do *not* abide by everything written in
the Law, whereas Paul's statement features those whose very identity rests upon "works of the Law." The most common solution to
this conundrum has been to suppose that an unstated premise
underlies verse 10: no human being *can* fulfill the Law perfectly and
consistently; thus even those identified by their commitment to the
Law stand, unavoidably, under the Law's own curse. Several obser-

vations weaken this supposition: Paul never (elsewhere) asserts that keeping the Law is impossible; moreover, whether it is possible to keep all the commandments is quite beside the point in the present passage; the implication that the Law cannot be fulfilled would be useless anyway, since even the agitators would agree that no one could keep the Law except with divine assistance, now available through the Spirit; besides, even if no one could obey the Law perfectly, the Law itself emphasizes God's forgiveness in response to repentance; finally, as Paul proceeds in verses 11-12 the issue is "doing" the Law, not an *inability* to do it.

In attempting to understand Gal 3:10 we must take seriously exactly what Paul says and what he does not say (as does Stanley 1990, 496-501). Paul writes: "For as many as are of works of the Law are under a curse, as it is written, 'Cursed everyone who does not abide by all things written in the book of the law by doing them' " (AT). Three features of the apostle's wording are noteworthy. First, in his quotation from Deuteronomy, instead of the LXX's "all the words of this law" (referring narrowly to the eleven proscriptions of Deut 27:15-25), he has "all the things written in the book of the law" (perhaps reflecting LXX Deut 28:58, 61; 29:20, 26; 30:10). Second, instead of adopting the scripture's term and declaring that *everyone* who is "of the law" is under a curse, he uses the word *hosoi,* "whoever, as many as," thus interjecting a note of indeterminateness. Third, and most significantly, Paul does not adopt from Deut 27:26 the verbal adjective "cursed." He writes instead that as many as are of works of the Law are *under a curse.*

This curse that persons are "under" is not the Law itself but rather the disasters that the Law forewarns will befall those who break the commandments. In Deuteronomy, as Paul well knew, the curse, like the blessing, is *conditional.* In chapter 27 (vv. 15-26) cursed (LXX: *epikataratos*) is anyone who does thus and so; in chapter 28 the people will be cursed *(epikataratos) if* they do not obey the Lord by keeping all his commandments (vv. 15-68). Indeed, *if* is one of the significant terms of Deut 27–30 (see 28:1, 2, 9, 13, 15; 30:16, 17). The Israelites are not cursed *because* they are a people whose charter is the Law of Moses. Rather, they are *subject to* the curse of God's punishment *if* they disobey that Law.

This is precisely what Paul means by his phrase "under the curse." "Under *x*" is a common expression meaning "subject to (the power or authority of) *x*." But to be subject to the curse of the Law is not to exist permanently and perpetually in a state of accursedness marked by disease and disaster. It is instead to be constantly exposed to the possibility of punishment if and when one transgresses God's commandments. In Gal 3:10*a* Paul did not—could not!—use the wording of his Deuteronomy quotation, "cursed" *(epikataratos),* because he did not want to say that persons of the Law were being punished by God. Thus, instead, his phrase "under a curse" means "subject to the Law's curse *if. . . .* " Paul's point is that the Law does not benefit its practitioners by supplementing or completing the work of the Spirit. Instead, it brings the threat of those punishments God will inflict upon anyone who fails to live up to its requirements. By pointing up this *disadvantage* of adopting the Law, Paul seeks to deter the Galatians from siding with the agitators.

Whereas verses 9 and 10 correspond in idea and language (albeit by contrast), verse 11*a* stands independent of what precedes, neither supporting nor further developing the thought of verse 10. It does, however, pick up again the "faith" and "justify" language of 3:6-9 (and 2:15-21). The apostle writes: "Now it is evident that no one is justified before God in [NRSV: by] the Law." Once again the locative sense of the preposition *en* predominates, so that "in the Law" is a designation of identity (as is "in Christ" at 2:17): persons who are "in the Law" are persons whose personal, communal, and social existence is defined and determined by the Law. What makes it "evident" that such persons are not justified before God is yet again scripture: "because the righteous one *by faith* shall live" (Hab 2:4 AT). For this biblical proof-text to work, we must assume that in Paul's thinking to "live" presupposes being justified, because "life" depends on God's favor. Whether he understands "shall live" to refer to present life (the seeming thrust of this whole passage) or to life following God's final judgment (as justified "in God's sight" or "before God [= God's judgment seat]" could suggest) is not clear.

Paul's quotation from Hab 2:4 differs from both the Hebrew ("the righteous one by his faith[fulness] shall live") and two different LXX manuscripts ("the righteous one by my faithfulness shall live" or "my righteous one by faith shall live"). As he quotes the verse, "by faith," set between subject and verb, can be read as attracted to "the righteous one" (thus: the one who is righteous by faith) or to "shall live" (thus: shall live by faith). Since he regards both as true, Paul would hardly object to either reading. He would object, though, to reading "the righteous one" in the Habakkuk quotation as a reference to Christ (as does Hays 1983, 150-57) because if Christ is "the righteous one," then the prophet's affirmation cannot serve to substantiate Paul's contention that *no one* is justified in the Law. The apostle has been talking about "those who believe" (3:7, 9), "the Gentiles" (3:8), "all who rely on the works of the Law" (3:10a), "everyone" and "no one" (10b, 11a). He provides his hearers no signal of any kind that he is shifting from "anyone/everyone" to Christ. Even though "the righteous one" in Jewish and early Christian literature can be a designation of the messiah, at Gal 3:11 it is generic and all-purpose.

The mere citation of Hab 2:4 will not convincingly demonstrate that no one is justified in the Law because, as many Christian Jews believed, the righteous person can live by faith *and* in the Law; a person can be righteous (justified) by faith and still take God's Law with full seriousness. And so Paul must argue that living "in the Law" is fundamentally incompatible with "faith." The purpose of verse 12, then, is to ground the claim of verse 11 with yet another, which Paul again verifies from scripture: "But the Law is not 'by faith'; rather, 'the one doing them shall live in them' " (AT). According to this quotation from Lev 18:5, those who "do" the commandments will find life by means of that doing. For Paul, however, in the last days persons "live" not because they obey the commandments but because of their response—he calls it "faith"— to what God has done, through Christ, to fulfill the promise to Abraham.

In response to this argument, Paul's theological antagonists might retort that Hab 2:4 and Lev 18:5 lack probative force because the apostle's use of those texts is transparently arbitrary. "Why not," they might ask, "rather conclude from the obvious truth of Lev 18:5 that 'the righteous one by faith shall live' *only* if the righteous one also obeys the commandments?" Clearly the priority that Paul assigns Hab 2:4 and his insistence on the incompatibility of faith and the Law are grounded in yet more fundamental convictions about the eschatological import of Jesus' death and resurrection. Those convictions underlie the affirmation of verse 13, an affirmation not connected syntactically with verse 12, but bound conceptually to verse 10. The first-person plural pronoun "us" now replaces the universal third person of verses 7-12, but Paul does not refer narrowly to himself and other Christian Jews. By "us" he means anyone who, wanting to belong to the people of the true God, would be subject to the curse of the Law; for if faith were not the means of standing in God's favor (being justified), no one would have any option except living "in the Law" (v. 11), and to live in the Law is, unavoidably, to make oneself subject to the Law's curse.

The Greek word usually translated "redeem" (v. 13), drawn from the sphere of commercial transaction, means to *purchase* and could call to mind the manumission of slaves. To this image Paul at once ties another that suggests *how* Christ's death is efficacious for others. This second image assumes the Galatians' familiarity with *pharmakos* rituals in Greco-Roman culture and lore: a designated figure takes upon himself a deadly curse and, by his expulsion or execution, discharges the curse, thereby freeing the community from its polluting power (McLean 1991). Even so, 3:13 is to be appreciated for its metaphorical power, not its theological precision. (To ask, for example, to whom the redemption price is paid would be to hear with a wooden ear.) Paul's metaphors provoke the realization that the ultimate source of the change he is speaking of, the change from being subject to the Law's curse to being blessed by God's favor, is not a matter of thinking or feeling or willing. The new life possibility he is describing *is* because something *happened*: Christ, in his death, *became* "a curse for us" (v. 13).

Paul supports the identification of Christ as "a curse" by once again quoting scripture. Deuteronomy 21:23, of course, does not even hint at his "for us"; that understanding of Jesus' death comes not from scripture but from early Christian theologizing. Particularly intriguing are Paul's modifications of the LXX Deuteronomy text ("accursed by God [is] everyone hung upon a tree"). He omits "by God," thus leaving unspecified the source of the accursed state.

He also changes the participle at Deut 21:23, *kekateramenos* ("[one who has been] cursed"), to the verbal adjective *epikataratos* ("accursed"), so that his scripture quotation at 3:13 features the same word as the quotation from Deut 27:26 in verse 10. The effect of this change is to dramatically characterize Jesus himself as one who did not "abide by all things written in the book of the law" (3:10*b* AT) and thus explain why the Crucified One incurred the Law's curse. In light of this freighted alteration, the apostle's wording in verse 13*a* is the more remarkable: Christ became not "accursed" *(epikataratos)*, the term in Paul's modified quotation from Deut 21:23, but "a curse" *(katara)*, the same term that appears in the phrase "under a curse" in verse 10. He surely means, though, that Christ became the *object* of the curse rather than the curse itself, the reason for this instance of metonymy remaining unclear (but see these parallel instances in the LXX: 4 Kgs [Heb 2 Kgs] 22:19; Jer 24:9; 33[Heb 26]:6; 51[Heb 44]:8).

The Deuteronomy passage from which Paul quotes at Gal 3:13 instructs the Israelites not to leave the body of an executed criminal hanging on a tree (or pole) overnight. The reason for burying him the same day as his execution is "because everyone who hangs upon a tree is accursed by God, and you shall not defile the land which the Lord your God gives you as your legacy" (LXX Deut 21:23). The criminal's body must be disposed of without delay because it pollutes the land, apparently because it is the object of God's curse. With his customary interpretive audacity, however, Paul claims that instead of polluting the land, by becoming a curse (that is, an accursed thing) Christ "bought us" from the curse of the Law, thereby freeing persons from the domain in which the Law's power to curse transgressors was in effect.

Important as it is as a clue to Pauline soteriology, Gal 3:13 is not an independent assertion. Indeed, in Paul's argument it serves primarily as the basis for the purpose clauses of verse 14: Christ "bought us" from the Law's curse "*in order that* in Christ Jesus the blessing of Abraham might come to the Gentiles, *so that* we might receive the promise of the Spirit through faith." Are these two purpose clauses sequential (the second logically dependent on the first) or parallel (both dependent on "Christ bought us")? According to the first option, Christ bought us so that the blessing of Abraham might come to the *Gentiles,* and the blessing of Abraham comes to the Gentiles so that "we" might receive the promise of the Spirit. According to the second, Christ bought us so that two events might happen concurrently. Recall that earlier Paul virtually defined being blessed along with Abraham as being justified the way Abraham was; thus the "blessing of Abraham" is the new status of being in God's favor, justified (3:6-9). Recall as well how closely Paul associates being justified and receiving the Spirit: for him neither is conceivable independent of the other. Recall, finally, that at 2:16-17 "through Christ-faith" and "in Christ" appear as parallel phrases modifying the verb "be justified." These recollections lead to the conclusion that the two purpose clauses of verse 14 are independent of, and parallel to, each other. Why, then, "Gentiles" in 14*a* and the more inclusive "we" in 14*b?* Perhaps because the "blessing of Abraham," claimed for generations by Israel, was a happening imaginable for *Gentiles* only "in Christ," whereas the bestowal of the Spirit was a novel happening of the last days for *all* believers, including, most emphatically, the Galatians.

In the second purpose clause of 3:14 Paul introduces an important new term in his argument: *promise.* By "the promise of the Spirit" he means the *promised* Spirit, the Spirit promised in the past and now poured out upon the Jesus-people. But promised where? In Scripture, Paul would surely say. But where in Scripture? And to whom? Such questions await an answer. For the moment, one can observe that by combining "Spirit" with "promise" in the very statement that introduces the term *promise* in Galatians, Paul is, in effect, defining the promise for his hearers: what was promised was the Spirit; the fulfillment of the promise is the outpouring of the Spirit.

The purpose clauses of 3:14 bring this part of Paul's "logical" proof full circle. He began by forcefully reminding the Galatians of their experience of the Spirit. He proceeded to note that their experience was akin to Abraham's being reckoned righteous because both his experience and theirs happened by faith, as indeed Scripture itself affirms. The way of the Law, fundamentally incompatible with the way of faith, subjects persons to its curse, but from that curse Jesus' death releases them. The "blessing of Abraham" and "the promise of the Spirit" summarize now what has happened through the death of Jesus in keeping with the gospel proclaimed beforehand to Abraham (3:8).

God's Promises and the Law (3:15-29)

At Gal 3:15 Paul again directly addresses the Galatians (this time as "brothers"), thereby marking another turn in his argument. "I speak," he says, "in human terms" (NRSV: "I give an example from daily life"), perhaps thereby signaling his hearers that in what immediately follows, the word *diathēkē* will not have its normal LXX meaning "covenant." *Diathēkē,* "last will and testament," will rather serve as a useful metaphor to highlight certain features of God's promise to Abraham. First, no one either cancels or adds to a human will and testament that has been formally validated (v. 15). Second, a will is a legal instrument whose purpose is the distribution of property to one or more specified beneficiaries. In the case of the "will" that Paul is here speaking of, "the promises were made to Abraham and to his offspring" (v. 16; literally: "and to his seed"). Paul knows as well as anyone that "seed" *(sperma),* in the Abraham story, is a collective noun: the patriarch's *many* descendants. In good Jewish exegetical fashion, though, he notes that Gen 13:5 and 17:8 do *not* read "and to your seeds" *[spermasin],* referring to many, but rather, referring to *one,* "and to your seed" *[spermati,* singular]; and that one seed is Christ (v. 16). In making this exegetical move, Paul's interpretation may not be as arbitrary as it first appears, for he is possibly drawing upon a tradition that understands the singular noun "seed" at 2 Sam [LXX 2 Kgs] 7:12 as the promised messiah. The *reason* for this emphasis on the singularity of the seed is not at once apparent. In fact, one's initial impression is that Paul's argument would proceed more smoothly if it moved directly from verse 15 to verse 17. Verse 16 seems to be an unnecessary interruption. Paul knows where he is headed, though, and in due time so will his hearers.

What does at once become clear is the reason Paul underscores (in v. 15) the unalterable nature of the will and testament as a legal instrument. "My point," he writes, "is this: the Law, which came four hundred thirty years later, does not annul a last will and testament [NRSV: covenant] previously ratified by God, so as to nullify the promise." That this is the case seems self-evident to Paul because the heir can receive his "inheritance" either by the instrument of Law or by the instrument of promise, but not by both. Which instrument, Law or promise, is consonant with Scripture is irrefragably clear: God has graciously given (NRSV: "God granted") the inheritance to Abraham through the *promise* (v. 18), Paul's verb *(kecharistai)* reminding his hearers of the key role of God's grace *(charis)* in the end-time drama of salvation.

The will and testament is a metaphor for God's promise to Abraham. Like a human will, that promise has in view a specified beneficiary, and like a will it cannot be altered once God has issued it, not even by the Law. One notable feature of verses 15-18 is the occurrence of the noun *promise* in both plural and singular forms (vv. 16, 17). Did God make one promise or several? By 3:18 Paul has quoted or alluded to three promises of God to Abraham: that Abraham's seed would be as numerous as the stars of heaven (Gen 15:5), the promise to which Abraham responded by trusting God (Gal 3:6); that all the Gentiles would be blessed "in" Abraham (Gal 3:8, quoting Gen 12:3/18:8); and that Abraham and his single seed would inherit the "earth" (Gal 3:16, quoting from Gen 13:15; 17:8; *gē* in these verses clearly means the "land" of Canaan, but Paul interprets the promise more grandiosely). On the other hand, at 3:14 Paul has virtually defined the promise (i.e., what was promised) as the Spirit. (Note that the word *promise* can either mean the pledge that does the promising [3:16, 17, 18, 21, 29] or the situation or event that fulfills the pledge [3:14, 22].) But where did God promise the Spirit to Abraham and his seed? As *we* read Genesis, we must answer, "nowhere." But Paul did not read Scripture as we do. I contend that he read the promise of many descendants, the promise of blessing to the Gentiles, and the promise of the earth *as* God's promise of the Spirit. What allowed this interpretation was Paul's conviction that the fulfillment of God's promises to Abraham was the work of the Spirit. Since only the Spirit could effect the blessings promised, the promises that Paul quotes or alludes to at 3:6, 8, 16 necessarily imply, for him, that God was simultaneously promising the Spirit. He can speak of "promises" (plural) because God promised the Spirit on more than one occasion and in different forms, but the "promise" (singular) is always either the pledge that promises the Spirit or it is what God promises, the Spirit (Williams 1988). At 3:18, in keeping with his will-and-testament metaphor, Paul introduces a synonym for the promised Spirit: *inheritance.* For the moment he does not explore the implications of this new term. His sole point is that God graciously gives the inheritance in keeping with the divine promise. The Law plays no role at all.

The Law/promise antithesis (vv. 17-18) brings to the fore a question lurking around the edges of Paul's argument since 2:15: What (or why), then, the Law? If the Law has nothing to do with granting the inheritance (3:18) or justifying persons (2:16; 3:11-12) or bestowing the Spirit (3:2, 5), if indeed the Law subjects persons to its curse (3:10), then what is the Law *doing* there, in the Scripture and in Judaism? Paul answers: "It was added because of transgressions" (v. 19). Added by whom? In light of the entire narrative of Exodus–Deuteronomy, one has no choice but to regard *God* as the subject concealed by the passive verb, and yet "added" gives the impression that the Law was somehow derivative, not part of God's original design. Certainly it was given subsequent to the promise—by 430 years, as Paul has just said (v. 17). "Because of transgressions" has provoked widely differing interpretations. One venerable and recurring view is that the Law was added to *produce* transgressions (e.g., Betz 1979, 165; Bruce 1982, 175; Räisänen 1983, 140-45), thereby calling forth God's grace as the only possible means of salvation. But nothing in the text of Galatians suggests this reading, and it must, in fact, appeal to another Pauline letter, Romans, for its principal support (see especially Rom 4:15; 5:20). "Because of transgressions," at least for the moment, remains open and indefinite. But whatever the Law's role and purpose, its function is a temporally restricted one, for the Law was added "*until* the offspring [seed] would come to whom the promise had been made" (v. 19). Until the coming of the single seed, the Law serves the purpose for which it was "added." How Paul understands Christ as the recipient or beneficiary of the promise, though, he does not explain.

Galatians 3:19 includes one additional statement about the Law: it was "ordered through angels by the hand of a mediator" (AT). Paul may be indebted here to a Jewish tradition attesting the role of angels in giving the Law at Sinai, but in no way does he imply that God is not the source and giver of the Law. The passive participle "[it was] ordered" and the prepositional phrase "through angels" leave no doubt about whom the Law originates with. And because the expression "by the hand of" *(en cheiri)* is so firmly associated in the LXX with Moses' role during the wilderness/Sinai period (e.g., Lev 26:46; Num 4:37, 41, 45, 49; 9:23; 15:23; 17:5; 36:13; Josh 21:2; 22:9; Judg 3:4), there is also little doubt that Moses is the "mediator" of 3:19.

Paul's next statement, though, defies a fully satisfactory interpretation: "Now the [or a] mediator is not of one, but God is one" (v. 20 AT). The affirmation that "God is one," the monotheistic credo of both Judaism and Christianity, is, of itself, not problematic. The puzzle it poses is its presence here: What purpose does it serve as the apparent counterpoint to verse 20a? The principal enigma of this verse, though, hinges on the word *one* in the first clause. Understanding the point and purpose of 3:20 requires deciding what this "one" refers to.

One possibility is that "one" is the single ("one") seed identified in 3:16 as Christ. In this case, Paul would be saying something like this: the Law was ordered through angels by a mediator (Moses). But the mediator does not belong to (literally: is not of) the one seed; that is, Moses is not among those who are "in Christ." Nevertheless, God is one. The advantage of this interpretation is that it understands "one" in the same way as the Greek word has already been defined by its context (3:16). Its main drawback is its inability to explain why Paul immediately adds, "but God is one." Perhaps his point would be that since God is one, God is God of both the mediator and the single seed, even though they are "founders" of different peoples.

According to a second reading, the "one" of verse 20a is the "one" of 20b—God, and indeed the principal purpose of 20b is to make clear that God is the "one" referred to in 20a. The mediator, Moses, does not mediate on behalf of one, God, but on behalf of many, the people of Israel, who, terrified by the Sinai theophany, begged Moses to speak to them in God's stead (Exod 20:18-21; Deut 5:22-27). Or, as the consecutive phrases "through angels, by the hand of a mediator" might suggest, Moses is an intermediary between Israel and the *angels* (who, in turn, represent God). In either case, by implication the seed to whom the promise was made, Christ, is superior to Moses. This interpretation nicely explains *why* Paul would have added verse 20*b*. The wording of this clause, however, is *not* most naturally read to mean "and God is [the] 'one' [i.e., the one just referred to in 20*a*]."

A third interpretation, preferred here, pays special attention to what Paul has just said in 3:19 about the Law's purpose, its duration, and the process by which it came to be. That process involves not just God, although it is God who "orders" the Law "through" and "by the hand of"; it involves angels and Moses as well. Verse 20*a*, though with obvious reference to Moses, is a *general* statement: a mediator of one does not exist—that is, the term "mediator" makes sense only in situations involving more than one party. If God alone were involved in giving the Law to Israel, there would have been no need for a "mediator." Thus the presence of a mediator is evidence that more than one party was involved. That other party was the angels. Furthermore, the sequence of the two prepositional phrases, "through angels, by the hand of a mediator," implies that Moses was in the immediate service of the angels rather than God. Thus, although Paul does not deny that God was the ultimate author of the Law, here he insists that the Law was issued through angels, and Moses was the instrument by which these messengers of God *(angeloi)* made the Law available to Israel. "But this mediator is not of one"—that is, at Sinai Moses was not working (directly) for a single party (i.e., God) but for a plurality (i.e., the angels), although God is indeed a single party. By so contrasting the singularity of God with the multiplicity of the messenger-beings who employed Moses to issue the Law to Israel, Paul deftly implies that the Law has a status different from that of the "inheritance" that God "graciously promised" (literally: "graciously gave through a promise," 3:18).

Does that mean that the Law is contrary to the promises? "Certainly not!" the apostle exclaims in reply (3:21).

Paul's exclamation seems at odds with his statements about the Law and the promises in 3:15-20. He asserts that the last will and testament (the promises being its "content") was officially validated "by God," but he does not add this phrase when he says the Law "was added." He says that God "graciously gave" the inheritance to Abraham through a promise, but he never makes a similar claim about the Law. Indeed, *God* is never the grammatical subject of any statement about the Law, and verses 19-20 seem intent upon underscoring the distance separating the Law and God. The assertions that the Law "was added" and that it arrived on the scene 430 years after the promise further emphasize the priority of the promises in Israel's history and in the divine design. Paul is certainly contrasting the promises and the Law. Yet he insists that the Law is not at odds with the promises. In fact, verse 21 implies, the Law and the promises even have a common goal: *life*. Nothing in the Law is contrary to God's purpose of giving life to the deity's human creation. Nothing in the Law is incompatible with the righteousness that is the basis of God's favor. If a law had been given that was *able* to make alive, righteousness would certainly be by the Law (v. 21). But that is not the case because the Law is not able to make alive. The Law cannot give life because by its very nature the Law is demand and not power. The law cannot *enable* God's people to do what it requires. It is not the enemy of God's purpose; it is not opposed to the promises of God. It is merely ineffectual. It cannot "make alive." But if the Law cannot give life, what can? To ask this in the context of the rhetorical questions that anchor this whole section of the letter is already to discern the answer: The Spirit gives life. Life, in its heavy "spiritual" sense, is the work of the Spirit.

In verse 22 Scripture makes its second appearance as an agent-surrogate of the deity in human history. At 3:8 Paul declares that Scripture proclaimed the gospel beforehand to Abraham ("All the Gentiles shall be blessed in you") because Scripture foresaw that God would justify the Gentiles by faith (3:8). According to Gal 3:22, Scripture "confined everything under sin" (AT). What Paul means is far from obvious, as the diversity of scholarly interpretations attests. Usually the phrase "under x" expresses the state of subjection to some power or institution. At Gal 3:22, though, sin appears to be not the authority in command but a subordinate that takes orders from Scripture. This does not mean that Scripture creates sin but that Scripture *uses* sin, once it is part of the human drama, for God's own purpose. But the apostle explains neither what God's purpose was during this confinement nor why Scripture put sin in charge. We must be content to note that Paul's image depicts sin as a power and that *confine* implies restriction or imprisonment. This confinement, however, is neither permanent nor, ultimately, purposeless: Scripture confined everything under sin *so that* what was promised might be given by Jesus-Christ-faith to those who believe. What was promised was, of course, the Spirit (3:14), the Spirit that does precisely what the Law is not able to do—that is, make alive (v. 21). Thus the very reason for Scripture's confining everything under sin was to ensure that faith would be the *only* means by which persons might receive the Spirit—and thus "life."

With his phrase "Jesus-Christ-faith," rather than simply "faith," Paul reminds the Galatians that he is not talking about faith as a general human possibility. He is talking about that distinctive life orientation which bears the imprint of Jesus Christ, that faith which Jesus inaugurated and now makes possible for those who are "in Christ." That Paul is talking about faith as an eschatological reality bearing the imprint of the Crucified One becomes unmistakably clear in verse 23. Some have read the articular noun "the faith," in light of 1:23, as a synonym for "the Christian message." It is preferable, however, to regard the article here as resumptive: *this* faith, the faith of verse 22, *Christ*-faith. This faith "comes"; it is "revealed." How so? Paul has once before used the apocalyptic verb *reveal* (1:16) and once before the verb *come* (3:19), each time with reference to Christ. This observation permits the suggestion that faith comes with Christ. In the last days, faith is present in the world first as the faith of Christ himself and then as the faith of those who are "in" him.

Now before this faith "came," the apostle writes, "we were held under the Law's custody, and thus confined, until the faith-to-be was revealed" (v. 23 AT). Paul's imagistic elaboration of his thought raises more questions than it resolves. His verb ("guarded, watched over, held in custody") and participle ("confined, shut up") are both passive, leaving open the question, "Confined by *what*?" "Held under the Law's custody" seems to imply that the Law is doing the guarding and confining. But the participle "confined" in verse 23 is a form of the same verb used in verse 22, and there it was Scripture that confined everything under sin. Thus Paul would seem to be equating the Law with Scripture. Yet he has earlier drawn a clear distinction between the two—Scripture foreseeing that God would justify the Gentiles by faith and proclaiming the gospel beforehand to Abraham (3:8); the Law, associated with neither faith nor the promise of God (3:10-12, 17-18), subjecting persons "in" it to a curse. Perhaps, then, we should assume that Scripture continues to be the real (but concealed) subject of the verb and participle of verse 23. Perhaps the Law is here *subordinate* to Scripture, the Law guarding and confining persons not of its own accord but at the behest of a superior authority. Thus it appears that, in spite of his seemingly parallel phrases "under sin" (v. 22) and "under the Law" (v. 23), Paul does not intend to equate the Law and sin; rather, both are subservient to Scripture, God's agent-surrogate.

The metaphor that very likely was already informing the language of verse 23, Paul makes explicit in verse 24: "Therefore the law was our *paidagōgos* [NRSV: disciplinarian] until Christ came, so that we might be justified by faith." In the culture of the first-century Mediterranean world, the *paidagōgos* was a member of the household, either a slave or a freedman with some education. He was responsible for the welfare of the master's son (or sons) from age six or seven until late adolescence. He accompanied his charge to and from (and at) school, the theater and lectures, the gymnasium and sports events, protecting him from any harm, including the designs of would-be male lovers. He supervised homework and meals and baths, gave instruction in manners as well as grammar and diction, and, ideally, both taught and modelled the moral virtues. Sometimes regarded with genuine affection by their charges, pedagogues were often strict disciplinarians, controlling the boys in their custody with threats, rebukes, and harsh physical punishment. But whether the pedagogue was loved or hated, his authority was, by its very nature, limited in extent and duration. He served at the pleasure of the master of the household, and his responsibility *as* pedagogue ended when his charge reached maturity (see Lull 1986, 488-95; Young 1987). The temporal limitation of the pedagogue's authority is the feature of this cultural institution that Paul draws upon in 3:25: "But now that this faith [i.e., Christ-faith] has come, we are no longer under a pedagogue" (AT). The Law came on the scene 430 years after God's promise to Abraham. With the coming of Abraham's seed, Christ, with the coming of Christ-faith, with the fulfillment of the promise, the epoch of the Law is over.

More than any other feature of 3:19-25, Paul's pedagogue metaphor helps to clarify his assertion about why the Law was "added" (3:19). To ensure the well-being of a child in his custody, a pedagogue might instruct, cajole, rebuke, or punish, but his constant aim was to guide and protect the boy whose welfare was his duty. By the very nature of the case, though, he had to severely restrict the personal freedom of his charge in order to fulfill his responsibility as pedagogue. So it was with the Law. The Law instructs and guides, rebukes and punishes, in order to protect from the harm that befalls any community of persons left to their own impulses, without law or custom or constitution. When Paul writes, then, that the Law "was added because of transgressions" (3:19), he is acknowledging that transgressions would have destroyed the people of Israel had it not been for the restraining role of that law—the Law of Moses—which instructed, rebuked, and punished. Nevertheless, his ambivalence toward the Law is evident, even the Law performing its intended function, in its own epoch. The verb and participle used in verse 23 to suggest its assigned role are two-sided. A soldier or jailer guards prisoners to prevent escape, but a parent (or pedagogue) guards children to protect them from harm; likewise, being confined can have a positive or negative sense: to protect or to restrict movement. In each case, though, what is common to both senses is the severe curtailment of personal freedom. The Law restrains and protects at great cost to its beneficiaries.

The "we" of 3:23-25 are all persons, Jews and Gentiles, who have stood before two ways, the way of the Law and the way of the promise, and have assumed the life-orientation Paul calls "faith"

(3:22). Now that this faith has "come," now that Christ has "revealed" faith, has made it a life possibility for humans in the last days, "we" are no longer subject to the authority of a pedagogue. "Indeed," the apostle writes, shifting from the first- to the second-person plural, "all of you are sons of God through faith, in Christ Jesus" (v. 26 AT). He does not speak here of "faith in Christ." Rather the last two phrases of verse 26 are coordinate, both describing how persons are "sons of God." "Through faith" specifies the means, "in Christ" the personal and social life-sphere into which believers are incorporated. Verse 27 confirms this reading of "in Christ": "As many of you as were baptized into Christ have clothed yourselves with Christ." The Galatians would have known what we can learn from Rom 6:4, that baptism was an immersion in water. The act signified a crossing of the real but invisible boundaries that defined the Christian community and distinguished it from those life-ways characteristic of the impure world. To be "baptized into Christ" was to experience a reconfiguration of one's symbolic world. It was to undergo relocation into a new order of existence created through the death and resurrection of Christ. It was to confess one's decision to be identified with—and by—Christ.

The theory that in verses 26-28 Paul is drawing from the liturgy of the baptism rite offers a way of accounting for the reference in verse 28 to slave and freeman and male and female, categories that seem to have nothing otherwise to do with Gal 3. On the other hand, this theory cannot so satisfactorily explain the distinctive Pauline language "baptized into Christ" (also Rom 6:3, and see 1 Cor 10:1) rather than the "baptized into the name of" formula that seems more typical of the early Jesus-movement (Matt 28:19; Acts 2:38; 8:16; 19:5; and the unavoidable inference to be drawn from 1 Cor 1:13-15). Perhaps, then, Paul here modifies the language of the baptismal liturgy, these verses having more the nature of a paraphrase than a quotation.

Another attractive theory holds that at verse 27*b* Paul draws upon the practice of new believers taking off their clothes to be baptized and putting them back on afterward (Meeks 1983, 151). But even if that practice could be verified for the Pauline congregations, it cannot alone account for the figure of "clothing yourselves" with *Christ*. Others have proposed that we find the closest parallel to Paul's metaphor in the "putting on" of a redeemer figure in the mystery religions and Gnosticism (Betz 1979, 188). When the texts cited are reviewed, however, the evidence that Paul could have borrowed this idea from either Gnosticism or the mystery religions turns out to be less than overwhelming. Either the texts are too late to attest ideas current in the mid-first century, or the alleged similarities are quite general.

To account satisfactorily for Paul's metaphor one need look no further than Scripture. Throughout the LXX Paul's verb *endyein* ("to put on," clothe oneself with, "wear") appears in an idiomatic figure of speech meaning "to be characterized by the named quality or attribute." God clothes himself with righteousness, majesty, power, and praise; that is, God's people experience and confess the deity as righteous, majestic, mighty, and worthy of praise (Ps 93 [LXX 92]:1; 104 [LXX 103]:1; 132 [LXX 131]:9; Isa 59:17; Wis 5:18). The psalmist prays that the priests of Israel be clothed with righteousness, and God clothes them with salvation (Ps 132 [LXX 131]:9, 16 [132:9, 16]; see also 2 Chron 6:41). When the prophet calls on Zion to clothe herself with her strength and glory (Isa 52:1; see also 51:9 in LXX), he is announcing that she will once more be a mighty, glorious city. And when, identifying with Jerusalem, the prophet declares, "He has clothed me with the garment of salvation" (Isa 61:10 LXX), he is rejoicing in the impending deliverance and restoration of the holy city (or nation). When God asks Job, "Did you clothe his [the horse's] neck with terror" (39:19 LXX), the deity is pressing the point that Job is not able to make so fearsome a creature. God gives human beings authority and "clothes them with strength" so that they might have dominion over beasts and birds (Sir 17:3 AT). Persons who clothe themselves with strength and dignity, with wisdom, with righteousness, are persons known by others as strong, dignified, wise, and righteous (Job 29:14; Prov 31:26; Sir 6:31). On the other hand, to be clothed with shame is to be humiliated in the sight of others (Job 8:22; Pss 35 [LXX 34]:26; 104 [LXX 103]:1; 109 [LXX 108]:29; 132 [LXX 131]:18; 1 Macc 1:28).

What makes the image of putting on a garment such an apt and useful figure of speech? A starting point for readers today is the realization that in the biblical world the face (and head), hands, and (often sandaled) feet were normally the only parts of a person's body that others saw. Much of a person's public appearance was the clothes she or he wore. Nothing except the face visually represented who and what a person was so much as did clothing. In the seaports and commercial centers of the Mediterranean world, clothes could announce one's country of origin, one's occupation, one's social class, or one's economic status. Clothing allowed people to discern what they had in common with others or how they were different. What would it mean, then, to say that those who have entered the Jesus-community have "put on" Christ? It means that differences that earlier might have separated them have now disappeared because everyone looks like Christ! Earlier Paul had written, "It is no longer I who live, but it is Christ who lives in me" (2:20). In 3:27*b* the figure is different, but the thrust of both is much the same: believers are so closely identified with Christ that Christ provides them the only identity, personal and social, that any longer counts.

In three short parallel clauses, verse 28 makes explicit the implications of Paul's "clothed with Christ" metaphor: "There is no longer Jew or Greek, there is no longer slave or free, there is no longer male and female; for all of you are one in Christ Jesus." Whether the last clause of this formulation draws upon a tradition of the primal human as an incorporeal and incorruptible *androgynous* being (Meeks 1974) is still a matter of dispute (see, e.g., Schüssler Fiorenza 1983, 211-14). Most students of Galatians do agree, however, that in shifting from "no longer . . . *or*" to "no longer male *and* female" (28*c*), verse 28 alludes deliberately to Gen 1:27 (LXX: "male and female he made them"). The formula thus envisions a state of affairs such as no one has ever seen, a situation superseding even God's original creation! Indeed, taken together, the parallel clauses of verse 28 describe a fundamentally changed human life-world. In society at large, distinctions that alienate (Paul spotlights distinctions of religion, social class, and gender) still define life and determine relationships. Those distinctions that nurture attitudes of superior and inferior, that encourage either resentment or indifference or arrogance toward the other, that allow domination and support the callous misuse of power—such distinctions still characterize the institutions of "the present evil age" (1:4). But in communities of persons who have clothed themselves with Christ these distinctions are honored no more. And so no longer can they grant privilege and prerogative to some while condemning others to impotence and indignity. No longer do they operate to separate persons from persons, "for all of you are one in Christ Jesus," *one* because all have taken on the appearance of Messiah Jesus.

The if-clause of verse 29 usefully clarifies the last phrase of 28: "and if you belong to Christ" (literally: "if you are of Christ") amounts to a rephrasing of "all of you are one in Christ Jesus." To be "in Christ" is to be "of Christ," to commit oneself and submit to Christ as his devoted servant-associate. So belonging to Christ, those who are one in him are now the seed of Abraham, heirs just as God promised (v. 29*bc*). With this affirmation Paul insists that in only one way can persons become Abraham's many seed and "heirs according to the promise": by becoming incorporated into Christ, the single seed of Abraham. The fact that this part of the argument culminates with an emphasis on Abraham's seed supports the view that "Who are the true descendants of Abraham?" was a key issue being pressed by the agitators. In summarizing his own position in 3:29, Paul echoes one of the principal terms of the foregoing section of the letter: *promise*. With this term he alludes again to the Spirit that the Galatians had experienced (3:2, 5; and recall the "promise of the Spirit" at 3:14); and with the term *heirs* he introduces the central theme of the passage to follow.

Heirs According to Promise (4:1-7)

With the first words of chapter 4 ("my point is this") Paul takes a breath, as it were, and begins the final part of his long central argument. As earlier at 3:15, he calls attention to a common legal practice that he can assume his hearers are familiar with. According to Roman law, a *paterfamilias* could appoint a guardian who would act on his son's behalf should the father die while the heir to his estate was still legally underage. Noting that legal practice in 4:1-2, in verses 3-7 Paul develops an analogy that allows him once more to underscore the new life situation of the "heirs according to the promise" (3:29). It is, however, only an analogy of sorts. Whereas "we" were actually enslaved (v. 3), an heir is "no different from" a slave (v. 1 AT). (Despite the NRSV, the subject in vv. 1-2 is singular). Paul cannot be making this latter statement with full seriousness, for even an underage heir enjoys privileges unknown to a slave, and they anticipate very different futures. In at least one way, though, their lots are the same: Neither is free to make substantive decisions on his own. And this is a point the analogy stresses: the heir "no different from a slave" and "we" who lived in an actual state of enslavement are both subject to authorities who curtail their personal freedom. But here the similarity ends. For although Paul characterizes both the heir and "we" as minor children (*nēpios* and *nēpioi*), he does *not* say that "we" were *heirs* during the period of nonage. In fact, according to verse 7, "we" (which has now become a singular "you") were previously *slaves*, not heirs, as "enslaved" in verse 3 has already said.

Enslaved to what? "While we were minors," Paul writes, "we were enslaved to the *stoicheia tou kosmou*" (v. 3). This phrase comes as a surprise, because earlier, in 3:23, "we" were guarded and confined under the *Law*. What relation is there, if any, between the Law and the *stoicheia tou kosmou?* The question would be easier to address if one could say with assurance what this phrase means. The basic sense of *stoicheia* is the fundamental elements of something, "something" being as diverse as language or matter. Thus in classical Greek and hellenistic literature the term can refer to the principles or components of a system, the stuff of which the world is composed, or the parts of the cosmos (such as stars). The context in which the word occurs usually makes its exact meaning clear, but that is not the case in Gal 4. Accordingly, we might assume that *stoicheia tou kosmou* was an expression already familiar to the Galatians from Paul's earlier preaching or conversation. Modern readers, not privy to that, must substitute whatever clues we can pick up from elsewhere in the New Testament.

In 2 Pet 3:10, 12 *stoicheia* (minus *tou kosmou*) refers to the elements of the natural world that will be consumed by fire on the day of the Lord, but the only other writing in which *stoicheia tou kosmou* occurs is Colossians, a letter written either by Paul or by someone who stood firmly in the Pauline tradition. The fact that Col 2:8 and 2:20 associate the *stoicheia tou kosmou* with human "tradition" and human "commands and teachings" inclines one to understand *stoicheia tou kosmou* in Col 2 as fundamental principles—religious and moral—of human behavior. So understood also at Gal 4:3, Paul's phrase would be broad enough to include the authoritative moral and religious traditions of both Jews and Gentiles and would thus, perhaps, correct the possible misimpression that only Jews were "imprisoned" and "guarded" before Christ came (3:23). With the addition of "of the world" to *stoicheia,* the apostle would be emphasizing, as does Col 2, that these religious and moral principles are the *world's* principles, merely human, and therefore their authority is not appropriate to the new situation created by the sending of God's son and the coming of faith. Their *intent* is salutary. They are even necessary to prevent social chaos. They nevertheless confine. Paul says they enslave—limiting, as they do, the possibilities of life.

One can, however, take a second approach and assume that since Paul does not (at 4:3) explain an expression that can bear such varied senses, that expression awaits clarification. And indeed, according to this view, in 4:8-9 Paul virtually defines the "weak and beggarly *stoicheia*" as "beings that by nature [or in reality] are not gods;" that is, those alleged but non-existent beings that the "sinners of the Gentiles" worship. But *is* Paul equating the two, the *stoicheia* and the non-existent deities? We recall that the "we" enslaved under the *stoicheia* at 4:3 correspond to the "we" guarded at 3:23 by the Law-pedagogue and must therefore at least *include* Jews. But how could Paul possibly be asserting that Jews were enslaved under beings that do not really exist? To escape this dilemma, one would have to propose that "beings who in reality are not gods" are demonic powers that do exist but are not really gods. If this is what Paul meant, though, he chose a singularly obscure way to say it. The most sensible alternative is the first view sketched above: *stoicheia (tou kosmou)* is a category broad enough to encompass the principles and practices of both Judaism and paganism. The worship of so-called "gods" (4:8) and the practice of the Law of Moses are two functionally equivalent ways of being subject to those religious and moral "fundamental elements" that Paul calls *stoicheia tou kosmou.*

Returning to the apostle's analogy, we observe that although the heir's state and status change, he has been a son all along. For those who were slaves, the change is more extreme: they became sons by adoption. Once his father has drawn up a writ of guardianship, the heir's situation changes inevitably, as a matter of course; his new life requires only the passing of time. With respect to his status as "owner of the whole estate," he can anticipate his future with aplomb, for he knows what will come to pass. The change of status from slaves to sons, though, does *not* happen inevitably, with the mere passing of time. It occurs because of a divine initiative, an act that snaps the bonds between dreary present and hopeless future and interposes a new and unthought mode of personal existence: the freedom and the prerogatives of sonship. Elsewhere in Galatians Paul stresses what Scripture foresaw (3:8) and what scripture foretells (e.g., 3:15-18); but here, from the perspective of those who were enslaved ("we"), he highlights the unplanned and disruptive aspect of God's initiative in sending his son. What has happened is "unnatural" and unexpected, the more so because God's son made purchase by his death (the same verb, *exagorazein,* occurs also at 3:13). The most notable difference between an underage heir and a slave is obvious precisely at this point. In verses 1-2 Paul "sets the stage" by describing the provisions of a testament of guardianship, but he does not describe what happens when the "date set by the father" arrives. By contrast, he devotes well over half the words of verses 3-7 to the new state of sonship, the event that made it possible, and the happening that attests its reality.

Who are the "we" who become sons? This passage raises again the problem of Paul's pronouns, especially since he moves so freely from "we" (vv. 3, 5) to "you" (plural, v. 6) to "our" (v. 6) to "you" (singular, v. 7). "We" can hardly be Christian Jews alone. In 3:26-29 Paul has just spoken of "you" as sons and heirs. He gives his hearers no signal at all that in 4:3, 6 he is speaking exclusively of (Christian) Jews. The view that he has only Jews in mind leads to chaos, particularly in verses 5-6. In that case, Paul would be saying, "God sent his son so that we Jews might receive sonship [a status long claimed by Israel!]. And because you Gentiles are sons, God has sent the Spirit of his son into the hearts of us Christian Jews . . . so that you (Gentile) are no longer a slave but a son." Paul certainly does not make things easy for his hearers in 4:3-7, but it is preferable to hold that "we" refers to all believers, Jews and Gentiles, whereas "you," while also inclusive, pointedly singles out the recipients of this letter, the Gentiles of Galatia.

Corresponding to "the date set by the father" in verse 2, "when the fullness of time had come" (v. 4) bespeaks a conviction about God's control of history that is at home in Jewish and early Christian apocalyptic thought. The apocalyptic schema does not become as explicit in Galatians as in other Pauline letters (see especially 1 Cor 15; 1 Thess 4:13-18), but Gal 1:4 has already indicated that it frames Paul's thinking about the Jesus-event.

The unusual nature of the expression "the fullness of time" (only here in Paul's writings), the apparent irrelevance to 4:1-7 of the participial phrase "born of a woman," and the alleged "sending formula" of verse 4 indicate to some commentators that in verses 4-5 Paul is drawing from an early Christian confession (Betz 1979, 205-8; Longenecker 1990, 166-68). Whether that be the case or not, he certainly articulates here the common Christian conviction that the central moment in God's dealing with humankind is the "sending" of his son. "Born of a woman" is an idiomatic way of saying "human being" (see Job 14:1; 15:14; 25:4; Matt 11:11; Luke 7:28; Josephus *Ant.* 7 §21; 16 §382); and to be "born under the Law" is to live the life of a Jew, a life shaped by Israel's constitution and guide. These phrases should not be read, however, as though the idea of preexistence was assured in the "sending" clause. That is, one strains to find here the affirmation that Jesus existed eternally with God, yet took upon himself the limitations of human existence in order to redeem humankind. Indeed, students of Paul's thought are not agreed about whether the preexistence of the son was a feature of Paul's Christology. Other texts regarded by some as evidence of this concept (Rom 8:3; 1 Cor 8:6; 10:4; 2 Cor 8:9; Phil 2:6-11) are subject to different interpretation. Certainly the verb *sent* does not necessarily bear the concept of preexistence. After all, scripture can use that language about prophetic messengers who were hardly thought to have preexisted their birth (Jer 7:25; Ezek 2:3; Hag 1:12).

God sends not only his son to liberate Jews and would-be Jews (like the Galatians) from the Law's restrictive authority. God also sends the Spirit of his son into the hearts of those who have been liberated. For Paul, son of Israel, the heart is the determining center of intellect and volition as well as emotion. Thus his affirmation in verse 6 is as much about the new sons' conduct as about their salvation—two subjects, in any case, that Paul never separates. "The Spirit of his Son," unique in Paul's letters, can hardly be other than the Spirit of God that has figured so prominently throughout chapter 3. The apostle cannot be claiming that believers receive the Spirit of God *and,* in addition, the Spirit of God's son. The exact connection he envisions between God's Spirit and God's son must remain, for us, unclear. We can only venture to say that Paul makes no discernible distinction between the power-presence of God's Spirit and the power-presence of the risen and exalted son.

Galatians 4:6-7 derives its force from the Galatians' own experience of the Spirit. At 3:5 Paul had mentioned miracles as evidence of the Spirit's presence. Now at 4:6 he declares that it is the Spirit *itself,* not Spirit-filled believers, that cries, "Abba! Father!" And, for people whose native tongue was Greek, the Aramaic word *abba* (deriving ultimately from Jesus?) carries an aura of the foreign and the extraordinary. These details of Paul's statements converge to indicate that receiving the Spirit was an experience of *ecstasy.* In the psychological jargon of our time, the early believers experienced a dissociative state. In their own language, they were filled with the Spirit; indeed, on these occasions of spiritual ecstasy, the Spirit was wholly in control, even of the human voice as it shouted out, "Abba!"

The argument of Gal 3:1–4:7 thus ends on the same clear note with which it began: the undeniable reality of the Spirit's powerful presence in the lives of the Galatians. What other evidence of sonship is needed than the Spirit-inspired cry, "Father!"? It is *"because* you are sons" that God sent the Spirit of his son into our hearts. Debate about whether the status of sonship precedes or follows the gift of the Spirit is irrelevant. Paul's point is that the experience of the Spirit is evidence of sonship, and, along with the miracles of 3:5, the Abba-cry is indisputable evidence of the Spirit's presence. "So," the apostle writes, shifting to the second-person singular to address each member of the Galatian assemblies, "you are no longer a slave; rather, you are a son; and if a son, also an heir, through God" (AT). The odd phrase "through God" occurs only here in Paul's letters. It is odd because "through" denotes means, whereas God is the very ground and source of redemption. The language is puzzling, but the thought is clear: all this is *God's* doing.

Paul's language in 4:1-7, as in most of chapter 3, is descriptive: "This is what has happened." But the apostle is not a theologian instructing the Galatians in the finer points of religious truth. He is a theologizing rhetorician aiming to change thinking, force decision, and shape conduct. The major rhetorical function of 4:1-7 is to force his hearers to acknowledge the absurdity of an adult "owner of all the estate" insisting that he be regarded once again as a legal minor, or the absurdity of an adopted son insisting that he return to the status of slave. Equally absurd, they should now realize, would be subjecting themselves to the Law.

Slaves No Longer (4:8-11)

The incredulity corresponding to this absurdity becomes explicit in 4:8-11, a passage providing transition from the argument of 3:1–4:7 to the appeal of 4:12-20. Sustaining the then/now schema of 3:23-29 and 4:1-7, verses 8-9*b* are descriptive of the Galatians' pre- and post-conversion states. The note of shocked disbelief in the rhetorical question of verse 9*c* bears a pointed rebuke reminiscent of 3:1 (and 1:6). Another statement (v. 10) reveals the fact responsible for the apostle's "fear" that his labor among the Galatians has been for nothing. With verse 11 Paul begins the appeal of 4:12-19, aiming straight at the feelings of his hearers by playing upon the bonds of friendship forged on the occasion of their initial meeting.

The language of "knowing" God and "being known" by God is highly reminiscent of Israel's Scriptures, especially the prophetic writings, where "to know" is a verb of relationship based upon encounter. For Israel to know the Lord is to acknowledge the Lord as God and to confess exclusive allegiance to this deity. (As representative "know the Lord" and "know that I am the Lord" texts, see Deut 4:39; 7:9; 29:6; Isa 19:21; 49:23; 52:6; Jer 4:22; 9:3; 22:16; 24:7; 31:34; Hos 2:20; 5:4; "they/you will know that I am the Lord" occurs over sixty times in Ezekiel.) When the prophets affirm that God has "known" Israel, they are speaking of the deity's election of, and covenant relationship with, this people. "You only have I known of all the families of the earth," declares the Lord through the prophet Amos (3:2; also Hos 13:4). To be "known" is to be chosen and blessed by God. In Gal 4:8-9, then, Paul is affirming that the Gentiles are no longer outsiders. They acknowledge and confess the true God; indeed, God has now "chosen" them as God's people. How incomprehensible, then, that they wish to retrogress to the status of outsiders, slaves to fundamental religious principles now superseded. "How can you turn back again [i.e., convert back] to the weak and beggarly *stoicheia?*" Paul asks in disbelief. "How can you want to be enslaved to them again?"

Verse 10 tells us what the Galatians were doing that Paul found so objectionable: "You are observing special days, and months, and seasons, and years." His reference, presumably, is to special times of worship and celebration according to the cultic calendar of Judaism. Coming as it does immediately after the question of verse 9, this exclamation implies that the religious observances pegged to a cultic calendar are among the "elemental principles" the Galatians wish to return to. Exactly which cultic occasions he refers to is impossible for later readers to know (especially since a number of feasts and festivals prescribed by Torah had to take place in Jerusalem), but Paul apparently feared that these practices would lead to the final step of circumcision.

◊ ◊ ◊ ◊

In *The Varieties of Religious Experience,* having averred that intuitions come from a deeper level of the self than the rational, William James declares:

> The truth is that in the metaphysical and religious sphere, articulate reasons are cogent for us only when our inarticulate feelings of reality have already been impressed in favor of the same conclusion. . . . Our impulsive belief is here always what sets up the original body of truth, and our articulately verbalized philosophy is but its showy translation into formulas. The unreasoned and immediate assurance is the deep thing in us, the reasoned argument is but a surface exhibition. (James 1902, 73)

Galatians 3:1–4:7 is clearly a reasoned argument. But we err if we think that Paul was a slave of Christ *because* he had become convinced by an argument such as he presents here. For the apostle, the "unreasoned and immediate assurance" that sustained him came from his Christ-revelation. And if the letter's recipients had not experienced the ecstasy and energy of the divine Spirit, we can assume that Paul's argument in Gal 3 would have had little chance to persuade them. This argument could convince, if convince it did, only because it resonated with the "deep thing" in them. That this section of the letter begins (3:2) and ends (4:6) by reminding the Galatians of their Spirit-experience is not fortuitous. Because they had received the Spirit by "the hearing of faith," Paul has grounds for confidence that they will hear his "spiritual" reading of Torah, a reading that discloses God's intent to bestow the Spirit on Gentiles like themselves. The argument of Gal 3:1–4:7, then, takes its hermeneutic cue from the Galatians' experience of the Spirit.

The Abba-cry (4:6) likely attests a Spirit-experience of ecstasy attendant upon baptism and the "crossing over" into a new life-world that it symbolized. The "miracles among you" (3:5) likewise give evidence that the Spirit was felt as an energy at work changing persons and their circumstances in ways not here specified. Paul's language (believers "receive" [3:2, 14], God "supplies" [3:5], God "sent" [4:6]) reveals his conviction that this energy was not a natural component or possession of the human being. It impacted

115

lives as something from without, something different from, and extraneous to, the self.

The work of the Spirit that this section of the letter both assumes and substantiates from Scripture is the creation of an inclusive human community, "heirs according to the promise" (3:29), Jews and Gentiles. In this vanguard of the new humanity that God is creating in the last days, identity markers that had served to separate and alienate persons—markers of race and religion, class and gender—have no more effect. They no longer block the kind of relationship that prevails among brothers and sisters who cry out "Abba" to the same father. Even though the Law itself sanctifies these identity markers, they now have no power because all who have received their inheritance are no longer subject to the Law's authority—or threat, or punishment.

A certain tension, however, marks Paul's stance. Although in Galatians we can discern his ideal of one inclusive human family, he does not say "all are sons of God" or "all are one." "You" and "we," not the unqualified "all" and "everyone," course through this passage. What Paul says is this: "All of *you* are one *in Christ Jesus*" (3:28); "all *of you* are sons of God *through faith, in Christ Jesus*" (3:26). His inclusive community, then, includes not everyone, without qualification, but everyone who has *faith*. The apostle's ideal is not shaped by the vague humanitarianism that is familiar to many of us. From his perspective, human beings of different races, different cultures, or different classes are not bound together by natural inclinations. They are family only as they are the children of one God, and they are God's children only as they acknowledge God, entrust themselves to God, and eagerly live in accord with God's will—that is, only if they have faith. They are brothers and sisters because they are "of Christ" and "in" him.

The metaphor of believers living "in Christ" is one of the most provocative in the letters of Paul. It belongs to one of the principal metaphor types by which we humans organize our life experience, the *container* metaphor. We speak of states or conditions as bounded spaces that we are either in or out of. Fundamental to the logic of this metaphor are the body-based distinction between interior and exterior and the notion of *boundary;* further, the metaphor depends on the bodily experience of being unable to occupy a space both inside and outside the same container at the same time (Lakoff and Johnson 1980, 29-32; Lakoff 1987, 271-73). Thus, entailing exclusion and restriction, boundary makes certain possibilities unavailable while ensuring others—most notably, some likeness or commonality with other subjects who are also "in."

In the metaphor "in Christ," "Christ" designates the domain in which believers stand justified (2:17), the domain wherein Christ is Lord. The logic of the empirical image (the human body in an enclosed space) carries over into the metaphor. Boundary remains key, as do the mutual exclusion of inside and outside and the giving up as well as the gaining of possibilities. One cannot be "in Christ" *and* "in (or under) the Law," and thus Paul's metaphor serves to identify Jesus-people by distinguishing them from the historic people of God. One cannot be "in Christ" *and* "under sin," and thus Paul uses his metaphor to distance Jesus-people from ungodly Mediterranean culture. The echo of rescue *out of* the present evil age (1:4) enables one to see that "in Christ" also suggests safe refuge. And "all of you are one in Christ Jesus" (3:28) highlights the power of boundary to effect a common bond—thus relationship, community, oneness—among those who are, together, inside.

As Paul uses the expression, "in Christ" has a clear social referent. Persons so identified are members of the Jesus-community. But the metaphor also bespeaks believers' communion with the risen Christ and thus presupposes Christ's resurrection. And as God's raising Jesus from the dead (1:1) reversed a natural state, so is "in Christ" an unnatural state for believers—above all, because in Christ's domain the enmities founded upon ancient distinctions of clan, class, and gender prevail no longer (3:26-28).

When Paul affirms that God raised Jesus from the dead, he is making a declaration absolutely central to his thought and his life. This is nevertheless a statement that differs in kind from the assertion that Jesus died. Again, "Jesus died for our sins" differs categorically from "Jesus died in Jerusalem." The latter belongs to the discourse of public event. The former does not. "Jesus died in Jerusalem" is a statement open to the modes of confirmation that humans take for granted in their everyday lives. But "Jesus died for our sins" is not. Nor is "God raised Jesus from the dead." Most of the statements of Gal 3:1–4:7 belong to this latter category of discourse. They are therefore subject neither to public verification nor to public disconfirmation. From an outsider's perspective, they reflect a *fictive* world of meaning. In more neutral terms, we can say that they reflect Paul's *symbolic* world. This world—which, for Paul, would incorporate the realm of "things not seen" (2 Cor 4:18)—intersects the world of public transaction at one crucial point: the socio-spiritual community of those who are "in Christ." This observation has enormous implications for Christian ethics and for the continuing mission of the church, because the only evidence of the realm unseen that many people will notice is the disposition and behavior of believers.

To be in Christ is to be liberated from the *stoicheia* of the world, whether the Law of Moses or beings who really are not gods (4:5, 8). It is easy enough for most Christians to agree with Paul's insistence that standing in God's favor, justified, does not depend on being circumcised or complying with the dietary regulations of Torah. But to agree with Paul is not to repeat his words or take comfort in the realization that food does not make one acceptable or unacceptable to God. Taking seriously his "not by works of the Law" requires Christians to attempt to discern what is *analogous* in their own time. The analogue, I contend, is not "legalism." That attempt at correspondence is too easy. What, rather, are the accoutrements of Christianity itself which, like the Law for Paul, can become slave masters? Doctrines meant to safeguard the integrity of the church's faith? Practices that keep outsiders out? And the "beings who in reality are not gods" (Gal 4:8 AT) but that many worship nevertheless, where shall Christians find *them* today? Incarnated as age-old prejudices and animosities? Camouflaged as political ideals? Ensconced on Wall Street? In the shrine of rampant consumerism? Between the covers of a holy book? Among the idols of popular culture? Seated proudly in the halls of academe?

In light of Paul's antithesis of (works of) the Law and faith, Christians also might well ask: How shall we identify *faith* in our day? Does faith require believers to embrace the cosmology or cultural values of another time and place? Must persons of faith assent unquestioningly to a particular set of truth-claims? Is faith allowed to be impatient of theological propositions? And if allegiance to principle should ever conflict with love, which of the two is faith's truest expression?

A Personal Appeal (4:12-20)

The "I" who moves to center stage in 4:11 becomes again in 4:12-20, as earlier in 1:6–2:21, a dominant presence in the letter as Paul now addresses his Galatian hearers directly. We find here an unusual concentration of epistolary conventions: a request formula (v. 12), two disclosure formulae (vv. 13, 15), and an instance of the vocative case (v. 19). The plural "you," in verbal and pronominal forms, occurs twenty-three times in verses 12-20; "I" or "me" occurs seventeen times; "we" appears not at all. Paul and the Galatians, even as "brothers" (v. 12), stand over against one another, as it were: Paul the object of their concern and goodwill in the past, they the object of Paul's present concern and urgent entreaty. Galatians 4:12-20 is, then, a fundamentally different type of discourse from 1:6–2:21 or 3:1–4:7. In the categories of ancient rhetoric, this passage is a "pathetic proof" (from *pathos:* emotion, passion). Rather than establishing his own character as credible and trustworthy (1:11–2:21), rather than weaving an argument of ideas and experience (3:1–4:7), Paul here plays upon the emotions the Galatians would associate with the joy and goodwill they felt on the occasion of his proclaiming to them the gospel.

The various sentences of this passage seem more disparate and disconnected than those of any preceding section of the letter. They are bound not so much to one another as to an underlying story of past relationship and present concern.

◊ ◊ ◊ ◊

Paul's appeal begins with the first imperative verb of the letter: "Become as I am" (4:12). His reason is surprising: "for I also have become as you are." This injunction strikes many modern readers as evidence of an unseemly arrogance on Paul's part. Perhaps it is. But the apostle can expect the Galatians to recall that he has presented himself as a slave of Christ (1:10) who, true to his initial experience of the risen Jesus (1:11-12, 15-16), has steadfastly defended the truth of the gospel (2:3-5, 11-14). More specifically, he has consistently refused to nullify the grace of God (2:21) by requiring Christian Gentiles to live according to "works of the Law," particularly circumcision and food laws. Paul has become like them in that he is a "sinner"; living by grace outside the Torah (2:17), he has given up his distinctive Jewish identity. They and he belong to God's family ("brothers") because of what *God* has done, and as evidence that they are sons and heirs, they have received the Spirit (3:2, 5; 4:6-7). When he pleads with them to "become as I am," he is saying: "Hold fast to the truth of the gospel as I do, for you are children of God *without* the Law."

Abruptly and without explanation Paul declares, "You have done me no wrong" (v. 12*c*). Presumably the Galatians knew exactly what he was talking about. We cannot know for sure; but if the conjunction *de* (v. 13) has the force of "indeed," the conclusion is close at hand that "you have done me no wrong" is his summary judgment upon their earlier treatment of him that he goes on to elaborate in verses 13-14: they did not "treat with contempt or 'spit on' what was a grievous trial for you in my flesh" (AT). The second verb here might be heard simply as a figure of speech meaning to disdain someone, thus a synonym of "treat with contempt, despise." It could, however, be taken more literally as a reference to the ancient practice of spitting to ward off sickness or demonic threats. In this case, Paul would be saying that the Galatians did not avoid him as one afflicted by demonic powers.

And what was the "grievous trial" in Paul's flesh that could have elicited such contempt and rejection? The apostle calls it a "weakness of the flesh" (NRSV: "physical infirmity"). His phrase has inspired numerous attempts at explanation, including malaria, epilepsy, poor eyesight, and physical debilitation caused by imprisonment or flogging. Once again, the Galatians knew; once again we cannot know, and again we do well not to mistake plausible proposals for historical facts. All one can say with some assurance is that Paul's "weakness of the flesh" was so offensive that contempt and rejection would have been very understandable reactions on the part of the Galatians.

Verse 13 strongly implies ("it was because of") that the reason for Paul's earlier proclamation of the gospel to the Galatians was not a long-planned missionary itinerary. It was, rather, his "weakness of the flesh." They would know whether the word *proteron* means "the first time" (if Paul had visited Galatia more than once) or, more generally, "earlier, formerly."

Verse 15 reminds us again of our disadvantage as non-Galatian readers. How shall we understand Paul's question, "Where, then, [is] your blessing?" (The NRSV has "What has become of the goodwill you felt?") The word *makarismos* can also be translated "happiness," and most interpreters hold that Paul refers to the initial exhilaration that the Galatians felt as a consequence of his preaching and their conversion, a blessedness they now risk forfeiting. This view assumes that "your *makarismos*" bears a passive sense: the Galatians' feeling of *being* blessed. Perhaps, though, Paul intends "your blessing" in an active sense: *their* blessing of *him* because he had been the human means of their coming to know God and receiving the wonder-working Spirit. This interpretation comports exceedingly well with verse 14 (they had welcomed him "as an angel of God, as Christ Jesus") and with verse 15*b*. In 15*b* Paul solemnly declares ("I testify"): "Had it been possible, you would have torn out your eyes and given them to me." This figure of devoted friendship and heartfelt appreciation illuminates "your blessing": they blessed Paul out of their affection and gratitude for the role he played in their conversion and new life.

Whether verse 16 be read as an assertion or as a question, it answers the query of verse 15*a:* the Galatians' blessing seems to have become a thing of the past. Paul has now become their enemy by telling them the truth (or, if v. 16 is a question, he senses this possibility). "Telling you the truth" refers, no doubt, to everything he is now writing in this epistolary offensive against the agitators, who are clearly the unstated "they" and "them" of verse 17. This verse is difficult to interpret because the verb *zēloun* (NRSV: "make much of") can have a negative or a positive or a specifically religious sense: to be jealous or envious; to strive for, exert oneself, be concerned about, or court someone's favor; or to manifest religious zeal, as did Phineas, Elijah, and the Maccabean defenders of the Law (Num 25:11, 13; 1 Kgs [LXX 3 Kgs] 19:10, 14; 1 Macc 2:24, 26, 27, 50). Knowing their own situation and the attitude and ploys of the agitators, the Galatians were in a much better position than we are to catch Paul's meaning, perhaps even his play on *zēloun* (which occurs three times in vv. 17-18—once with the agitators as subject, once with the Galatians as subject, and once in a general adage). Paul's accusation seems to be that the agitators have zealously sought the Galatians' favor and assent to their views, but not in an honorable way; "rather, they want to shut you out, so that [as a result] you are zealously seeking their favor" (v. 17 AT).

"Shut you out" raises, for us, the question, "From what?" The answer most in keeping with the immediate context is: from the circle of Paul's friendship and influence, in order to enhance their own influence. Another possibility, though, is that the agitators want to shut them out of the people of God—*unless* they eagerly seek the favor of the agitators and agree with their view of the gospel. "It is good," the apostle says, "to be zealously courted in a proper way—*always,* and not just when I am present with you" (v. 18 AT). The barbed implication of this statement is that the agitators' methods and motives have been less than admirable in his absence. Doubtless these Christian missionaries would beg to disagree, but we have no letter from their pen. We see them only through Paul's partisan eyes.

The appeal of 4:12 Paul now grounds unobtrusively in a figure that implies the Galatians' dependence on him for their very life as believers (v. 19). His metaphor, though, appears to be confused. The Galatians are (already) "my children," and yet Paul is a woman in labor trying to give them birth. Giving birth to a child is a one-time event, yet Paul is in labor with the Galatians *again.* The plural pronoun "whom," the grammatical object of the verb *ōdinein* ("to be in labor, suffer the pain of childbirth"), refers to the *Galatians,* yet Paul is again in labor not until *they* are born but rather "until Christ is formed among you" (or "in you" [so NRSV], i.e., in your lives, just as "in me" at 2:20 means that Christ lives in Paul's life).

The passive verb "be formed" can provide an initial insight into the idea finding expression in the metaphor of a woman giving birth. Who is the actual subject concealed by the passive form of the verb? Who is responsible for Christ "taking shape" in the Galatian congregations? Not the Galatians themselves. Not even mother Paul. It is rather *God* who is doing the "forming," the One who sent his son in the first place (4:6). A second insight comes with the realization that in the prophetic writings "like a woman in labor" is a well-worn simile for the intense suffering that will befall Jerusalem or Judah (or her enemy) as the consequence of God's judgment (Isa 13:8; 21:3; Jer 4:31; 6:24; 13:21; 22:23; 30:6; 48:41; 49:22, 24; 50:43; Mic 4:9-10; also Sir 48:19). Readers of the Bible alert to the "narrative of divine purpose" that shapes the prophetic oracles know, however, that God's judgment prepares the way for God's *deliverance.* Thus the suffering of God's people betokens their salvation, a hope made explicit in several of the texts just cited (Isa 13:1–14:2; Jer 30:4-11; Mic 4:9-13). Indeed, the most startling use of this simile occurs in a salvation oracle of Isa 42. Here *God* declares, "For a long time I have held my peace, I have kept still and restrained myself; now I will cry out like a woman in labor, I will gasp and pant. I will lay waste mountains and hills. . . . " So will God deliver the Judean captives in Babylon (Isa 42:14-17). We do not find the simile "like a woman in labor" at Gal 4:19, nor do we find anything approximating an oracle of judgment. We find instead a metaphor—Paul *is* a woman in labor—which, like the prophetic simile, suggests momentous changes being wrought by God as the deity forms and fashions an altogether new order of existence, "Christ formed among you." With another metaphor, that of dying with Christ, Paul has already affirmed how this (trans)formation takes place (2:19-20), and his emphasis on the Spirit makes clear the power that makes it possible.

In verse 20, using again the verb of verse 18, Paul avers, "I wish I were present with you now and could change my tone," thereby acknowledging the inevitable limitations of a letter read to the assemblies by someone else. He is confident that his personal presence among them would make unnecessary the harsh tone of this communication. At a distance he is "perplexed about you," but if he were present he could assess the situation for himself and more effectively activate the affection that would override the appeal of the agitators.

◊ ◊ ◊ ◊

Galatians 4:12-20 can remind readers of Galatians that commitment to "the truth of the gospel" does not rest solely on the persuasiveness of reasoned argument. Remembered emotions of joy and gratitude and the powerful bonds of friendship can play their own important role.

Paul notes that although his physical affliction was a "grievous trial" for the Galatians, they had not treated him with revulsion or disdain. They had instead welcomed him as though he were an envoy of the deity, even as Christ Jesus, probably because of the message that he bore. Indeed, the fact that, in spite of his affliction, they welcomed him as they did tells us much about the captivating power of the gospel he preached.

Paul has not yet used the word *new* in Galatians (it occurs only at 6:15), but the idea of the unprecedented permeates the letter. With the metaphor of himself as a woman in the agony of giving birth, the apostle focuses attention on both his missionary labor and his certainty of its result. But although Paul labors, it is God who does the creating. What God is working at is an altogether new order of existence, not by creating a new heaven and a new earth (as in Revelation) but by "forming" Christ in the lives of believers. When the Galatians recall that Christ is the model of self-giving love (2:20), they can anticipate what their lives and communities will look like when Christ has "taken shape" in their midst.

An Allegory of Two Women (4:21–5:1)

In this passage Paul offers an allegorical reading of Abraham's two sons and their mothers; these biblical personages he transmutes into types, prefigurations of two covenants and their "children." By alternating third-person description (vv. 22-26*a*, 29-30) with "we" and "you" statements (vv. 26*b*, 28; also 31), he uses the Genesis story to speak directly about, and to, the Galatian situation.

A vocabulary distinctive of Galatians holds the passage together semantically and binds it to earlier parts of the letter: *slave girl, slavery,* and *serve-as-a-slave* (vv. 22, 23, 24, 25, 30, 31; see 4:1, 3, 7, 8, 9); *free[woman]* (vv. 22, 23, 30, 31; the same word, but probably as an adjective rather than a noun, appears in v. 26); *promise* (vv. 23, 28; see 3:14, 16, 17, 18, 21, 22, 29); and *flesh* (vv. 23, 29; see 3:3). *Spirit,* occurring only once in this passage (v. 29), recalls 3:2, 3, 5, 14 and 4:6; and *inherit* in the quotation from Isa 43:1 (v. 30) reminds the hearer of *heir* and *inheritance* at 3:18, 29 and 4:1, 7. With respect to vocabulary, the chief development in 4:21-30 is Paul's emphasis on the word *free[woman]*. This word (as noun or adjective) is not to be found earlier in the letter, and the noun *freedom* has appeared only at 2:4. Now this term takes center stage, and the spotlight falls on it alone at 5:1, where Paul virtually shouts, "For *freedom* Christ has set us free." The pairing of contrasting entities (slave girl/freewoman, flesh/promise, present Jerusalem/Jerusalem above; in slavery/free; flesh/Spirit) provides the structure of the passage.

4:21-31: For several different kinds of reasons one suspects that it was not Paul who introduced the Genesis accounts of the birth of Ishmael and Isaac into the discussion, that it was, rather, the agitators. Even when we consider the license characteristic of the figurative interpretation of scripture in Paul's time, the way he stands the "two sons" material of Genesis on its head (in Jewish tradition Isaac was the ancestor of God's people and Ishmael the father of outsiders) attests an audacity that seems prompted less by his own interpretive imagination than by circumstances. Whereas in 3:1–4:11 Paul had spoken of a single covenant centered on God's promise to Abraham, here we find him contrasting *two* covenants, and this in spite of the fact that Genesis contains nothing about a covenant with *Ishmael* (although in Gen 17:20 God does promise Ishmael blessing and numerous posterity). Furthermore, these Genesis passages are too *dangerous* for Paul to have brought into the conversation unless he felt forced to. They are dangerous because they interweave the accounts of the births of Abraham's two sons (Gen 16–17; 21:1-4) with God's command to *circumcise.*

Finally, two somewhat more technical clues: Usually in Paul's letters "it is written" introduces a direct quotation from scripture (as, for example at 3:10, 13; 4:27). At 4:22, however, Paul does not quote scripture; rather, in verses 22-23 he gives a brief interpretive *synopsis* of Gen 16–18; 21. Nor does he think it necessary to name either sons or mothers at the beginning of his interpretation (indeed, he never does name Sarah or Ishmael). These two facts suggest that the Sarah-Isaac/Hagar-Ishmael stories of Genesis were already, prior to his writing of the letter, part of the conversation between the Galatians and the agitators.

In the context of Jewish convictions likely shared by representatives of a Law-observant Christian mission to Gentiles, we can assume that the agitators found in the Genesis stories indisputable sanction for circumcising all "sons of Abraham." Torah allowed no male to belong to the people of God who had not undergone this rite. At God's command Abraham himself had even circumcised Ishmael, along with every other male in his household (Gen 17:23-27). If one argument of the agitators ran along these lines, it is obvious that Paul was forced to offer a counterreading of the Genesis stories in his attempt to undermine their case. In this attempt, the virtuosity he displayed as a "scripture expert" would perhaps have had as great an effect as the actual persuasive power of his claims.

Paul begins his counterreading with an assertion that no one could possibly dispute: Abraham had two sons (that Abraham later had six more sons [Gen 25:1-2] was a scriptural fact irrelevant to either side). His characterization of Hagar as a "slave girl" is likewise unobjectionable, for the LXX regularly describes her as a *paidiskē* (literally, a young girl, but in our literature the term connotes slave status more than age; see LXX Gen 16:1, 2, 3, 5, 6, 8; 21:10, 12, 13). On the other hand, the word Paul uses to characterize Sarah, *free(woman) [eleuthera],* is not used of Sarah in Genesis. Nevertheless, no hearer could possibly object. The biblical stories clearly depict her as a freeborn woman (indeed, the Hebrew name *Sarah* means "princess"). But although unobjectionable on the basis of the Genesis text, Paul's characterization of Abraham's wife as a *"free(woman)"* is a shrewd move because "free" becomes the crucial center of this whole passage—and of the exclamation to which it is tending (5:1). The "spin" that Paul is putting on Genesis is equally clear in verse 23, for Genesis never alleges that Ishmael was born "according to the flesh" or Isaac "through the promise." But, once again, who could object to Paul's language? Genesis records that, at Sarah's suggestion, Abraham had sex with her slave girl; Ishmael, then, is the offspring of a union that is in no way extraordinary. Not so Isaac. He was begotten when Abraham was one hundred years old and Sarah was ninety (Gen 17:15-21; 18:1-12); and in light of the divine promise that Sarah would bear a son (Gen 17:15-16, 19; 18:10), the Lord's question to Abraham at LXX Gen 18:14 ("Shall what was spoken [the promise] be impossible for God?") unmistakably implies God's participation in Isaac's begetting. So far, we can assume, Paul and his antagonists would be wholly in agreement.

The first hint of what prompts the rebuking challenge, "Will you not listen to the Law?" comes in verse 24: "These things are to be interpreted figuratively" (NRSV: "this is an allegory"). The verb *allēgorein* (from *allo* and *agoreuein*: "to speak otherwise") means to speak or interpret in such a way that words bear a meaning other than their literal sense. In the Greco-Roman world this was a widespread method of interpreting sacred or traditional texts, among Jews and non-Jews as well. In thus announcing his hermeneutical strategy, Paul gives notice that he will read scripture subversively—that is, in a way that subverts the agitators' case. His first move comes in verse 24, not when he declares that the slave girl and the freewoman represent two covenants, but when he links Hagar, slave girl who bears children into *slavery*, with Mt. *Sinai*, the sacred mountain on which Moses had met God and received the Law. Earlier Paul had spoken of the Law's power to confine (3:23) and had affirmed that Christ redeemed those who were subject to the Law's authority; but the language of *slavery* he had associated with the "elements (of the world)" (4:3, 9) rather than directly with the Law. Now, in 4:23, he becomes unmistakably direct: adherents of that religious system that had its origin at Sinai are no less slaves than was their "mother," Hagar.

Galatians 4:25a has so puzzled interpreters that some have considered it a scribal gloss, but it is no easier to explain what would prompt this parenthesis from a later scribe than it is to explain why Paul would interject it. The manuscript evidence reflects the puzzling nature of the comment. The earliest and thus most authoritative manuscripts are split between two readings: "[This] Mt. Sinai is in Arabia" (or "[this] Sinai is a mountain in Arabia") and "this [name] Hagar is [i.e., refers to] Sinai in Arabia" (or "this Hagar-Sinai mountain is in Arabia"). Is Paul here displaying his interpretive virtuosity by playing on the similar sound of the Hebrew (and Greek) name *Hagar* and an Arabic word for "rock" or "cliff" that could be used to refer to a mountain? The probability that the Galatians would not be familiar with this Arabic word (and thus would not be able to appreciate Paul's pun) does not necessarily disqualify this explanation of verse 25a, for Paul had earlier informed them that he had spent time in Arabia (1:17), and he might have regarded the word *Arabia* in verse 25 as a sufficient clue that he is engaging in a wordplay that they cannot themselves confirm. (I note, in passing, that the word *Arabia* occurs in the NT *only* at Gal 1:17 and 4:25.) Anyone familiar with Genesis should, in any case, be prepared to accept Paul's association of Hagar with "Arabia" because the Genesis narratives place her and Ishmael in desert regions (Gen 16:7-14; 21:8-21). Another, and perhaps preferable, solution to the puzzle seeks to make sense of 25a in light of the rest of the verse. "Now this 'Hagar' refers to Mt. Sinai in Arabia; but (nevertheless) she corresponds to present-day Jerusalem." According to this interpretation, Paul's point would be that the geographical locale of Hagar-Mt. Sinai (in Arabia) is no barrier to his associating Hagar with Jerusalem (in Palestine).

Having just identified the Hagar-Sinai covenant as a system of slavery (4:24), in verse 25 Paul declares that the "children" of Hagar-Jerusalem serve as slaves. Thus those who define themselves by their allegiance to the Law are not free persons. But over against present-day Jerusalem, represented by Hagar and her enslaved children, Paul sets the "Jerusalem above" represented by the freewoman; and she, he says, "is *our* mother," the mother of all Christians. This affirmation is not materially different from the claim that Christians are begotten according to the Spirit (4:29): their birth is due to no earthly power but to the creative power of God. To be children of the present-day Jerusalem, though, is to be limited to the natural, the merely human; and circumcision is a sign of that "fleshly" existence (see "born according to the flesh" as the opposite of "born according to the Spirit" at 4:29).

The formula that introduces the quotation from Isa 54:1, "for it is written" (v. 27), indicates that Paul intends for the prophet's words to provide biblical support for something just said, but the exact connection between the quotation and what precedes it is elusive. The quotation's emphasis is a call to rejoice, but Paul has said nothing about rejoicing, and the logic of his Sarah/Hagar allegory does not fit the logic of the quotation. The prophet's words set forth the "barren," "desolate" woman and "the woman who has the husband" as *contraries*, whereas in Genesis it is the woman *married* to Abraham who was for a long time barren. Isaiah 54:1 does not yield a perfect match with Paul's reading of the Sarah/ Hagar story. So why does he quote it? What claim does it support? Points of contact between the quotation and its context are by no means missing. "Barren" *(steira)* certainly describes Sarah before the birth of Isaac in her old age. Furthermore, Paul well knows that with the images of a "desolate" woman and a fruitful married woman the prophet speaks of Jerusalem in ruins and Jerusalem restored, so the *Jerusalem* motif also connects verses 27 and 26. But although these points of contact might *allow* the quotation, they hardly explain what *prompts* it. The "fit" that evokes the quotation seems to be its connection with the current situation in Galatia rather than with Paul's Hagar/Sarah allegory.

"She is our mother" (v. 26) implies the birth of children, and the birth of children is a reason to rejoice (v. 27*a*). The prophet's call to rejoice is especially appropriate in Paul's own day because the freewoman, Jerusalem above, has brought forth numerous off-spring, that is, *converts*—"many more" than the woman never barren has produced. Her own previous barrenness symbolizes the fact that those who are now her children had not earlier belonged to the covenant community whose "husband" was the Lord (see Jer 3:6-13; Ezek 16; Hos 2). This cause for rejoicing is due to the miraculous work of the Spirit. The Spirit's begetting of many children (4:27*b*-29) fulfills not only the prophet's words but, as well, God's promise to Abraham that "all the Gentiles shall be blessed in you," that is, as Abraham's children (3:8). You Gentile Christians, Paul says, are the children of promise, the children God promised Abraham (4:28).

Who, then, are the children of the other woman? Are they non-Christian Jews? The word *persecute* in verse 29 seems to favor this view. Paul uses this same term to describe what he had done to the "church of God" (1:13), and we can assume that he was not the only zealous Jew sufficiently offended by the Jesus-movement to respond with "persecution" (see 1 Thess 2:14-15, which makes the point even if 2:14-16 is a gloss; the author of Acts, too, knows the tradition of Jewish persecution of Christians [14:2, 5, 19; 17:5, 13]).

Self-evident as it seems, however, the view that Hagar's children symbolize non-Christian Jews becomes less certain when one takes note of a minor but significant feature of Gal 4:21-31: the participle that Paul uses in verse 24, "bearing children." The verb here is *gennan*, which occurs also in verses 23 and 29. This verb can mean "beget" or "bear," but in the LXX it usually describes the part of the *man* in procreation; another verb, *tiktein*, normally describes the part of the woman. In the Genesis (LXX) stories of Ishmael's and Isaac's birth, the verb used of both Hagar and Sarah is consistently *tiktein* (16:1, 2, 15; 17:19, 21; 18:13; 21:2, 3, 7). This is also the verb in the first line of the Isaiah quotation at Gal 4:27. Why, then, does Paul "replace" this verb, in verse 24, with a verb that in the LXX describes the role of the male? Two other occurrences of *gennan* in Paul's letters are quite suggestive. At 1 Cor 4:15 Paul writes to his Corinthian "children": "In Christ Jesus I myself begot you [NRSV: became your father] through the gospel"; and at Phlm 10 he speaks of "my child, Onesimus, whom I begot [NRSV: whose father I have become] during my imprisonment." In these instances "begetting" is a metaphor for creating new Christians through his missionary preaching. (The Galatians, of course, had read neither 1 Corinthians nor Philemon, so they would not be aware of the connotation of *gennan* in those letters. But unlike us, they do not need that evidence. They *know* whom Paul is referring to.) It follows that the slave girl who births children into slavery (v. 24) symbolizes missionaries who insist on works of the Law—that is, the Galatian agitators (Martyn 1991).

This identification makes excellent sense of 4:30. Here Scripture makes its third and last appearance in Galatians as God's surrogate-agent in the drama of the deity's unfolding purpose (see 3:8, 22). Adapting them to his theme of freedom, Paul invests Sarah's words to Abraham (LXX Gen 21:10: "Cast out this slave girl and her son, for the son of this slave girl shall not inherit with my son Isaac") with new authority by transmuting them into a command of *Scripture* to the Galatians: "Cast out the slave girl and her son, for the son of the slave girl shall not inherit with the son of the free[woman]" (AT). Appealing to Scripture's own voice, then, Paul pointedly instructs the Galatian Christians to expel the agitators and their "children," those who have adopted their views and yielded to their demand for circumcision. As contemporized by the apostle, the scriptural command to "drive out the slave girl and her son" can hardly be heard as anything other than a ringing iteration of the *anathema* that Paul had earlier pronounced against anyone who preaches a message incompatible with the gospel the Galatians had heard from him (1:8-9).

According to this interpretation, the persecution of verse 29 ("so it is now also") would be the harassment and pressure tactics of the agitators rather than the sort of persecution that Paul himself had engaged in (1:13, 23). The major advantage of this view lies in its ability to illuminate the command from Genesis 21:10 as the principal goal toward which the whole passage aims.

In 4:31 Paul's "so then" does not introduce a conclusion that has only at this point emerged. Verse 31 does not offer any new information. It serves two other purposes. Its "children" casts a glance back at Abraham's two sons and summarizes what Paul has been claiming throughout the intervening passage 4:21-30—namely, that Christians free from the Law correspond to Isaac and that those who are "enslaved" to the Law correspond to the slave girl's son. This terse summary of who Paul's Galatian converts *are*—free persons—then prompts an affirmation of *how* they came to be free, an affirmation that reminds his hearers of the "Christ redeemed us" declaration of 3:13-14: *Christ* has set them free.

5:1: Verse 5:1 can be regarded as the center of Galatians. This letter begins with an emphasis on the one gospel of Christ (1:6-9). Paul later recounts how he defended the *truth* of this gospel against false brothers who attempted to undermine the "*freedom* we have in Christ Jesus" during his second visit to Jerusalem (2:1-5). His allegory of the two mothers in 4:21-30, the slave girl and the freewoman, has now prepared the way for him to articulate the truth of the gospel in terms of freedom: "For freedom Christ has set us free," he exclaims. This exclamation, the most forceful *declaration* in the letter, then grounds the letter's central injunction: "Stand firm, *therefore,* and do not submit again to a yoke of slavery" (emphasis added). Paul clearly signals the centrality of this command and the exclamation that grounds it. Although 5:1 is connected thematically with what precedes and follows and indeed functions as a bridge passage between the allegory and the parenetic material of chapters 5 and 6, syntactically this verse stands in grand isolation. No particle or conjunction binds it to what precedes, and no conjunction or particle in 5:2 connects verse 1 to what follows.

The word *again* is puzzling. Paul is writing to Gentile, not Jewish, Christians. How, then, could they be said to be getting caught *again* in a "yoke of slavery"? Two answers are possible: (1) The "yoke of slavery" refers not to the Mosaic Law alone but to any form of the *stoicheia tou kosmou* to which the Gentiles had been enslaved. (2) Although the Galatians to whom Paul directs this appeal had not yet allowed themselves to be circumcised, earlier, as God-fearers, they had observed a number of the commands of Torah, so that adopting the views of the agitators now would indeed be getting caught *again* in the Law.

◊ ◊ ◊ ◊

Paul's proclivity for dichotomies, so obvious in earlier parts of the letter, finds expression again in 4:21-31. The fundamental opposition here is slave/free, and because it has not occurred earlier in the letter the word *free* (used, with one possible exception, as a noun: *free[woman]*) is particularly striking. The *idea* of freedom has, of course, shaped earlier passages, most obviously 4:1-7, but it is the exclamation of 5:1 that elevates it as the centerpiece of Galatians.

What Paul has written thus far is enough to warn us that our ideas of freedom are not the same as his. His notion of freedom has little in common with Western ideals of individualism and self-determination. Recall some of the phrases that he would put in the column opposite freedom: under sin (3:22), under the Law (3:23; 4:5), under a pedagogue (3:25), under trustees and managers (4:2), under the "elements of the world" (4:3 AT). The antithesis of these states would certainly seem to be personal autonomy. But one needs to recall as well that their alternative is life "in Christ." To be in Christ is to belong to Christ (3:29), to be subject to *his* lordship. To be in Christ is also to be drawn into a *community* of believers who are responsible to and for one another.

If Paul himself can serve as an example, freedom means abandoning violence as a way to rid the world of values or beliefs that threaten one's own (1:13-14). It means release from the religious and cultural prisons whose darkness breeds prejudice, suspicion, and resentment (3:26-28). As enslavement to Christ, freedom is also an indifference to "pleasing" people (1:10). Humans expend enormous amounts of energy on the project of gaining the approval of others in order to secure the self against self-doubt and vague suspicions of worthlessness. Freedom is liberation from the enervating effort to protect the *egō* from the hurt of others' judgment. Since the effort to protect and the desire for approval normally require a goodly portion of self-deception and dissembling, freedom from these compulsions allows the vulnerable honesty that is conducive to genuine human relationship.

In Gal 3 and 4 Paul associates the state of being free with the promise, the Spirit, and faith. Faith is the necessary condition of freedom. It is only as persons relax in divine grace, entrusting themselves to God in utter confidence, that they can give up every attempt to justify themselves before God. Believers rest assured! The *power* that creates freedom is the Spirit, for it is the Spirit that transforms outsiders into members of the family of God. According to Paul's allegorizing interpretation, only "children of the promise" are free because only they are *heirs,* begotten by the Spirit. But perhaps freedom and promise are connected in a more fundamental way than by the story Paul reads out of Genesis. By its very nature, any promise can be kept only by the person who made it. Only the promiser can determine the destiny of promise by ensuring its fulfillment. Accordingly, a promisee is not in control—unless, of course, the promisee *forces* fulfillment, in which case the operative dynamics are no longer those of *promise.* Though dense with possibility, then, freedom, in the context of promise, is a condition of loss and absence. Where promise prevails, I am not in charge. I am a beneficiary who cannot effect my own benefit. I am, as we say, completely at the mercy of another. But in this loss of control I can for the first time experience my existence and all that sustains it as sheer gift. It is fitting, then, that my liberation comes not through my own effort but through the death of another who was free enough to love and give himself up for those still unfree. "For freedom Christ has set us free!"

That Paul reads the Abraham story as a veiled prefiguration of the church is nowhere more obvious than in Gal 4:21-31 (Hays 1989, 105-21). It is hardly fortuitous that *freedom* takes center stage in a passage that, in the wake of 3:26–4:7, so clearly assumes an inclusive *community* as context for the life of faith. For Paul, freedom is not independence. It is, rather, openness to the risks of connectedness and mutual dependence.

Does the freedom that Paul claims in Christ also entail exemption from hermeneutic restraint? Galatians 4:21-31 raises the question as sharply as any passage in the Pauline letters. Any reader of Galatians who is also familiar with Genesis will likely be struck by what nowadays can be called the apostle's strong misreading (Hays 1989, 115). Even an awareness of the allegorical interpretation of Homer and the Jewish Scriptures (particularly by Philo) in the hellenistic era does little to reassure many readers that Paul is not taking undue liberties with the Genesis text. In Paul's hands, it seems, scripture has become a ventriloquist's dummy (Shaw 1982, 44).

Even if that language is excessive, Paul's counterreading of Genesis does raise an important question about the responsible use of Scripture. If Christians find in the Bible what they already stand convinced of on other grounds, how can the Bible be for them the word of God that unsettles and reorders life's priorities? On the other hand, does not the history of biblical interpretation, both popular and professional, confirm what Paul's counterreading implicitly admits—namely, that Scripture cannot secure its own interpretation because a universal hermeneutical point of reference is not available? Christians inclined to censure Paul might ask themselves this question: If the Bible is to be a living word and not merely an antiquarian relic of interest only to historians, how can Christians *avoid* appropriative strategies that, in *principle,* do not differ from Paul's? But if they admit such strategies, how can Christians assure themselves that they are not listening to the echo of their own voices?

Richard Hays thinks we must credit Paul with some ironic sensibility as Paul flips the story of Abraham's two sons on its back (Hays 1989, 112). Readers of Galatians who can agree will perhaps discern in Gal. 4 a certain serious playfulness in the apostle's reading of Scripture. If so, they may be able to entertain the possibility that a decorous solemnity may not always afford the most fitting way to hear a word that promises liberation and life.

Faith Working Through Love (5:2-12)

Having defined the Galatian Christians as "children of the freewoman" by his subversive rereading of the Sarah/Hagar story (4:21-31), having declared the means by which they became free, and having urged them not to revert to their previous state of slavery, Paul now, in 5:2-12, reinforces his plea in two ways: first he appeals to his hearers' own spiritual self-interest (vv. 1-6), and then he takes a final slap at the agitators as he moves from rhetorical question (v. 7) to an imprecatory exclamation of savage humor (v. 12). An unusual concentration of sentences without conjunctions or transitional particles marks verses 7-10. Nevertheless, the assertions and questions that make up this section are not disjointed.

What connects them, however, sometimes lies below the surface of the text.

◊ ◊ ◊ ◊

As Galatians is read publicly, its hearers will hardly have forgotten who wrote it. Yet the emphatic "I, Paul" serves forcefully to remind them, and thereby to intrude Paul's presence into the gathered congregations. Ignoring his appeal will be more difficult, and the cause of greater discomfort, if the voice and visage of the letter's public reader do not replace the voice of the apostle. Implicit in the warning that follows ("if you let yourselves be circumcised, Christ will be of no benefit to you") is the assumption that Christians "believe" because they are concerned for their ultimate well-being. Indeed, rhetoricians would designate verses 1-6 a "pathetic appeal," that is, an effort to persuade by emphasizing the advantage or disadvantage following upon some course of action.

If verse 2 asserts what Christians who submit to circumcision would lose, verse 3 declares what they would get in return: an obligation that deprives them of the freedom Christ offers. Freedom is the chief *benefit* that Paul is presently emphasizing, and the *loss* of freedom makes one a "debtor" who must do the whole Law. The similar sound in Greek of "will benefit" *(ōphelēsei)* and "debtor" *(opheiletēs,* NRSV: "obliged") subtly reinforces the magnitude of the exchange. Paul's solemn legal-sounding language ("I testify") and the present tense of participle ("who lets himself be circumcised") and verb ("is") make the apostle present as if the rite were being performed, and there he issues this stern warning whose purpose is precisely to prevent that from actually happening. Whether Paul is asserting that the person circumcised must then keep every prescription of the Law perfectly at all times in order to be approved by God remains an open question. His point is that anyone who accepts circumcision can no longer adopt only those Jewish practices that he finds attractive (such as the religious observances mentioned at 4:10). Circumcision is the ritual of entrance into a distinctive people, and one who takes that step takes upon himself the obligation to live according to the Sinai covenant in every sphere of personal and communal existence. He adopts a complete way of life. In doing so, however, he severs himself from that inclusive community where ethnic distinctions remain but are no longer in effect (3:28).

The obligation the Galatians stand to "gain" Paul states, in verse 3, as a general principle and in the third person. Verse 4 returns to direct address, and the sentence's emphasis falls on its initial and final words, verbs translated "you . . . have cut yourselves off" and "you have fallen away" by the NRSV. The precise nuance of the initial verb, *katargein,* is especially difficult to determine. Its root, *argein,* means to be idle, unoccupied or at rest, to do nothing. When the prefix *kata* is added (basic senses: down, toward, opposite), the meaning of the resulting word (which occurs in the NT almost exclusively in the Pauline corpus) seems to be "to make ineffective." The following preposition *apo* ("from, away from"), however, does not easily fit that sense. We can, then, hear the clause as an abbreviation for "you have come to nothing as a result of separating yourselves from Christ"; or we can allow the force of the preposition, in effect, to modify the sense of the verb: "you have gotten released from Christ" or "you have been removed from Christ's jurisdiction, from the sphere of Christ's operation" (see Rom 7:2, 6, where the passive of *katargein* plus *apo* means "to be released or removed from the jurisdiction of the Law"). In any case, the sense of separation and dislocation is clear in the sentence's final verb: "you have fallen out of grace" (AT).

Unlike those who "fall out of grace" by heeding the agitators' appeal, steadfast Christians (Paul includes himself in the emphatic "we" that begins v. 5) eagerly await "the hope of righteousness." This NRSV translation accurately reflects the ambiguity of Paul's Greek phrase. Does he refer to an unspecified reward that being right with God allows Christians to hope for? Or does he refer, rather, to the righteousness that Christians hope for, this hoped-for righteousness being God's verdict of acquittal at the last judgment? The parallel expression "the promise of the Spirit" (that is, the promised Spirit) at 3:14 favors the second interpretation. It is true that in Gal. 3 (6–9; 14), righteousness seems to be the *present* state of being right with God, but this observation does not obviate the "hoped-for righteousness" reading of 5:5. As the immediately preceding statement makes clear, Paul's confidence that Christians have been justified does *not* mean that they cannot still turn their backs on God. "Be justified" does not describe an irreversible transaction. *Dikai*-root terms always have to do with relationship, and relationship is affected by conviction and behavior. One *can* foolishly remove oneself from Christ's sphere; one can "fall out of grace." The Christian life, therefore, remains, for Paul, *goal* oriented.

The phrase (v. 5) "through the Spirit, by faith" recalls the Galatians' experience of receiving the Spirit by "the hearing of faith" (see 3:3, 5) and points to the "external" and "internal" sources of believers' existence. Faith is that personal receptivity to God's grace that allows the Spirit to be at work in believers' lives, and the Spirit's power sustains them as they await God's judgment with eager anticipation.

Verse 6 grounds the warnings of verses 2-4. Gentile believers do not need to take up the Jewish way of life (v. 3). What binds them together is their common allegiance to Christ, not the Law. The boundary markers that define the Christian community and distinguish it from the wider society issue not from the Law, as in Judaism, but from Christ. In this community neither circumcision nor uncircumcision makes any difference; both are irrelevant. This assertion of apparent indifference about circumcision surprises in light of what precedes (especially 5:2). Paul would surely say, though, that the Galatians had misunderstood him if they were to respond, "Well, if neither circumcision nor uncircumcision matters, why not get circumcised—as Abraham did?" (Gen 17:23-27). His point is that one's identity as Jew or Gentile, circumcised or uncircumcised, has nothing to do with one's standing with God. The only thing that matters is "faith working through love." "Working" *[energoumenē]* is the participial form of a verb used twice previously of *God's* activity (2:8; 3:5), but here it is the faith of believers that "works," although earlier Paul had insisted that faith and works *(erga)* of the Law were contraries.

Significantly, the apostle does not write, "What matters is faith." Instead, as he begins to turn from an extended discussion of how persons become the people of God (sons of Abraham, heirs, "in

Christ") to a description of that community's distinctive character, he emphasizes the social and communal *manifestations* of faith. The *character* of Christian community is love *(agapē)*. Paul's hearers will recall that earlier he had spoken of "the *faith* of the son of God who *loved* me and gave himself up for me" (AT). If this rendering of 2:20 matches Paul's intent (that is, if he did not mean "faith *in* the son of God"), then one notices a close parallel between that verse and 5:6. Galatians 2:20 does not state explicitly that Jesus' act of self-giving was the outworking of his faith, but Paul's affirmation is certainly open to such an understanding. In any case, the model for the love through which faith makes itself effective is Christ himself. Previously (4:19) Paul had expressed the desire that Christ would "be formed" among the Galatian believers. In 5:6 he begins to specify how that is to happen.

Galatians 5:7 does not match the harshness of "you foolish Galatians!" at 3:1, but it is a rebuke nevertheless. "You *were* running well" unmistakably implies that they are running well no longer. For the second time in the letter (see 2:2) Paul relies on the athletic metaphor of the foot race, but here it is an image of the Christian life, not of his missionary work. The image is particularly apt at this point because it brings to mind ideas of *exertion, freedom* (runners were unencumbered because they stripped and competed nude), and *purpose* (the finish line was the runner's goal and reason for competing), and Paul has just characterized the Christian life as faith "working" through love (5:6); he has also just reminded the Galatians of the goal and reward that Christians eagerly await (5:5). He continues the running image with the question, "Who cut in and got in your way so that you are not continuing to obey the truth?" (AT). The truth is, quite specifically, the truth of the gospel that Paul had himself so stalwartly defended at Jerusalem and Antioch (2:5, 14). The infinitive just translated "to obey" *(peithesthai)* means, in the active voice, to *persuade,* but in the passive voice (as here) it has a wider semantic range: be persuaded, listen to, obey, comply with, believe, trust, rely on. The translation "obey," then, is somewhat misleading because it conveys only one of the passive verb's several aspects. One needs to be aware that the verb also bears the connotation of relying on and complying with what one has been persuaded by.

The "persuasion" that is keeping the Galatians from relying on the truth of the gospel does not come from God (v. 8). It comes from the agitators, of course, but Paul's assertion might hint that they are but instruments of a higher power, Satan himself. "The one who calls you" echoes 1:6. God calls both Gentiles and Jews out of this present evil age into a new human community. The agitators' views now threaten the distinctiveness of that community. Indeed, as he shifts abruptly from his athletic metaphor (running) to a *baking* image, Paul likens the effects of those views to the power of a small amount of yeast. His aphorism, "a little yeast leavens the whole batch of dough," carries a warning and an injunction. It is this implicit injunction, in fact, that connects verses 9-10 with 7 and 8. The warning is this: The agitators constitute a threat to the well-being of Christian community that, if not removed, will permeate and drastically alter the very nature of the church. In light of the *anathema* of 1:8-9 and the scripture quotation at 4:30 (from Gen 21:10), verses 9-10 amount, as well, to another call to expel the agitators. Expulsion, then, is at least the initial punishment that "whoever it is that is confusing you" will have to bear. ("At least" because Paul's language could also suggest to his hearers God's final judgment: the agitators will not attain the hoped-for righteousness [v. 5].) In light of 1:7 ("some who are confusing you"), "whoever it is" must refer not to one person alone but to all the agitators, each of whom will "pay the penalty" no matter what his status or authority or personal charisma might be. The generic singular functions rhetorically to disparage the agitators while forcing each member of Paul's audiences to name them for himself or herself.

In spite of the past tense verbs of verse 4 and the rebuke of verses 7 and 8, in verse 10 Paul affirms his confidence that the Galatians will, finally, see things his way. The ground of his confidence is his and the Galatians' common allegiance to the lordship of Christ ("in the Lord"). By "not think otherwise" Paul means, in the first place, that he is certain the Galatians will agree with the implication of his maxim, namely, that a small bit of mischief can cause great harm. In the second place, he is confident that the Galatians will agree that each of the agitators must bear his judgment. If the Galatians "catch" Paul's meaning and agree that the teachings of the agitators would irreversibly alter the inclusive Christian community, they will, he hopes, accept the responsibility of driving out of their communities the latter-day sons of the slave girl (4:30).

Why in verse 11 Paul intrudes a rhetorical question about *himself* is not obvious. He appears to be contrasting himself with the agitators, but because of our distance from Paul and the Galatian situation, we lack the information that would allow us to hear verse 11 as the Galatians did. Evidently the apostle is responding to the allegation that as a Christian missionary he insisted on circumcision as a requirement for Gentiles who desired to belong to the people of God. The "still" in the question's if-clause acknowledges that in some earlier period of his life he *had* "preached circumcision." Most likely that was before, rather than after, "God revealed his son in me" (1:16 AT), for the New Testament contains no evidence that as a Christian missionary Paul ever insisted on Gentile circumcision. With the question, "Why am I still being persecuted?" he exposes the absurdity of this charge. What we cannot know, however, is what underlies the charge. Were the agitators claiming that Paul elsewhere insisted on Gentile circumcision but altered his message to the Galatians in order to ensure a greater number of converts? Had those making the charge seriously misunderstood earlier statements of apparent *indifference* to circumcision (such as those at Gal 5:6!)? Did they consider Paul inconsistent because he did not object to circumcision among Jews but insisted that Gentile converts *not* be circumcised? Were they familiar with a report (such as the one underlying Acts 16:1-3) that as a *Christian* Paul had been responsible for the circumcision of Timothy, a man whose mother was Jewish but whose father was Gentile? Perhaps the Galatians knew the answers to such questions, but once again we do not.

Paul does not describe how he is still being persecuted or by whom; but since he is being persecuted because he is no longer "preaching circumcision," his persecutors must be non-Christian Jews or conservative Christian Jews. He declares that to require circumcision for Gentile converts would be to nullify the *skandalon* of the cross (the verb, a favorite of Paul's, occurs also at 3:17 and

5:4). The word *skandalon* is rare in non-biblical Greek literature. In the LXX it translates the noun derivatives of two different Hebrew verbal stems, "to catch in a trap" and "to slip or stumble," and can thus mean "a trap or snare" (e.g., LXX Ps 139:6) and "an obstacle that causes one to stumble" (e.g., LXX Lev 19:14). The term can therefore be a metaphor for that which occasions transgression or destruction or that which causes opposition, revulsion, or offense. The second sense predominates here. Not only does Paul set the "*skandalon* of the cross" in sharpest antithesis to the requirement of circumcision; he seems almost to revel in the offense that the gospel of Christ crucified causes. Why should this be so? Apparently because of the close connection in his mind between Jesus' redemptive death and God's creation of an inclusive community consisting of Jews and Gentiles who remain Gentiles. The abhorrent nature of crucifixion serves to underscore the social distinction of this community, those who have died with Christ, from those who still belong to the present evil age.

In verse 12 Paul exclaims: "I wish those who have gotten you all stirred up would cut themselves [*apokopsontai*] off!" (AT). His exclamation is subject to various interpretations. One can hear these words as a wish that the agitators, who had "cut in" [*enekopsen*] on the Galatians (5:7), would now remove themselves from the Christian community. But anyone who recalls the language of Deut 23:1 [LXX 23:2] would know that in that verse "cut off" refers to severing the penis. Since Paul has just mentioned circumcision (v. 11), his verb in verse 12 could well bring to mind a botched circumcision: he wishes that the knife would take not the foreskin of Gentile converts but the whole penis of each of the agitators! (The image of a bungled circumcision does *not* well fit the act of cutting off the testicles. Thus modern translations that render Paul's verb "castrate," as well as the view that the force of v. 12 derives from a traditional ridicule of eunuchs in the hellenistic diatribe, are, at best, questionable.) The severing of the penis would, of course, cut a man off from the people of God according to Deut 23:1. Paul's exclamation well expresses the frustration he feels, the anxiety and anger caused by the agitators' threat. His savage humor caricatures the rite that they insist Gentiles must submit to, and the letter's recipients might realize the absurdity of holding that one cut of the knife can incorporate a person into the people of God while another can exclude him (Dunn 1993, 284).

◊ ◊ ◊ ◊

As a synopsis of the Christian life, no phrase in Paul's letters is more revealing than Gal 5:6: "faith working through love." The import of this phrase becomes clearer when we note the different "directionality" of faith and love. Although Paul can speak of God's (or Christ's) love for humans (Rom 5:5, 8; 8:35, 37, 39; 2 Cor 5:14; 9:7; 13:13; Gal 2:20; Phil 2:1[?]) and humans' love for God or Christ (Rom 8:28; 1 Cor 2:9; 8:1[?], 3), the noun *agapē* and the verb *agapan* most frequently name a disposition of persons toward other *persons*, a disposition expressed in conduct (Rom 12:9; 13:8, 9, 10; 14:15; 15:30[?]; 1 Cor 4:21; 13:1-13; 14:1; 16:14, 24; 2 Cor 2:4, 8; 6:6[?]; 8:7, 8, 24; 11:11; 12:15; Phil 1:9[?], 16[?]; 2:2[?]; 1 Thess 1:3; 3:6, 12; 4:9; 5:13; Phlm 5, 7, 9). This is certainly the case in the three later occurrences of the term in Gal 5 (vv. 13, 14, 22). Even though God's love, or Christ's, is the source and paradigm of human *agapē*, this term most frequently names a disposition creative of human-human relationship. "Faith," however, is that disposition of the self necessary for humans' relationship with God. To schematize the point: in Paul's theological vocabulary, *faith* is a "vertical" term; *love,* most frequently, a "horizontal" one. We might also say that, as a "private" matter between a person and God, faith is closed to public viewing. What evidence, then, can faith give of itself? Paul says: *love. Agapē* is the public evidence of a right relationship with God because faith, the human disposition necessary for such relationship, manifests itself and has effects through love. Now what if one should say to Paul: "But what about a faith that does not express itself through love?" The apostle's response would be, I think, "You are not talking about *faith* at all." "Faith" that does not materialize as love cannot sustain a relationship with God because it knows nothing of One who, in the fullness of time, sent the Son who "loved me and gave himself for me" (2:20; 4:4-5). Faith is that response to God's initiative that opens the gates of the self to God's transforming power. The faith of which Paul writes, then, is not locked in the spiritual closet of one's private transaction with God. It erupts into communal life as love.

Called to Freedom, Led by the Spirit (5:13–6:10)

Most of Paul's letter to the Galatian churches has had, thus far, one principal aim: to persuade the letter's recipients to reject the overtures of the agitators. To this end he has pressed into service historical narrative, theological argument, personal appeal, and direct exhortation. With 5:13, however, the apostle turns from the threat of the agitators to the threat of the "flesh." This move is not so considerable as it might appear, since the agitators preach the different gospel that requires the sign of God's covenant "in your flesh" (1:6 and 3:3; Gen 17:13). Nevertheless, in this passage Paul's purpose is not so much to dissuade the Galatians from getting circumcised as to recall them to those patterns of conduct that befit Christian freedom from the Law and the (other) *stoicheia*. The dominating verbs of 5:13–6:10 are imperatives and hortatory subjunctives, and even Paul's declarative sentences (notably 5:17-24) serve his ethical injunctions. In their relation to one another, these directives appear discrete, sometimes even disparate. Many do not seem distinctively Christian, since one can easily cite parallels from Greco-Roman literature. Yet they all have the crucified Christ as their model, and the actions enjoined are, for Paul, the kind of fruit the Spirit bears in the lives of believers freed from the yoke of the *stoicheia,* whether the Law or so-called "gods."

Set Free to Love (5:13-15)

Verse 13 restates the letter's key affirmation, the ringing declaration of 5:1, in order now to clarify what Paul means by "freedom" and what he does not mean: *not* a freedom that would provide a base of operation, an occasion and pretext, for the flesh. The NRSV's translation of "flesh" as "self-indulgence" (main text) clouds the multiple connotations of this important term. In the previous part of the letter it has referred simply to the human being (1:16; 2:16, 20) or to the human being constrained by the limitations and weakness of creaturehood (4:13-14). But for Paul's hearers it would also carry echoes of his deprecating remark about circumcision (3:3). It might also bring to mind the way Paul disparages the merely natural ("born according to the flesh") by associating Hagar and her modern "descendants" with slavery, while identifying Christians, on the other hand, with God's promise and the working of the Spirit (4:23-25, 29-30). "The flesh" could signify both Jewish ethnicity and sexual desire (Boyarin 1994, 68). In any case, at 5:13 "flesh" assumes a decidedly negative sense, without which the instruction implicit in this verse would not be comprehensible. Here Paul speaks of "flesh" as a power that can take advantage of the freedom God gives and can use that freedom for its own unloving purposes. "Flesh" has its own "desire" (5:16), engages in inevitable conflict with the Spirit (5:17), and produces its own "works" (5:19-21), works that contrast sharply with the "fruit" of the Spirit (5:22-23).

Paul envisions freedom not as a natural right but as a divine gift. God has *called* Christians to live free, but freedom is not a good in itself. It is rather a *means* to the great good of human relationship. Freedom is not untrammeled personal autonomy. It is, rather, opportunity and possibility—the opportunity to love the neighbor without hindrance, the possibility of creating human communities based on mutual self-giving rather than the quest for power and status. The very key to the proper use of freedom is love, for it is love that enables persons to give themselves as slaves to one another (5:13-14).

Paul's command to the Galatians to use their freedom to make themselves one another's slaves is startling, not only in light of his previous remonstrances against slavery to the *stoicheia* but also in view of the ideals of the age. Philosophers denigrated people's "slavery" to their fears, passions, and possessions; they praised autonomy and calm detachment from such entanglements. In sharp contrast, Paul enjoins the Galatians to *enslave* themselves. But unlike the institution of slavery in the Greco-Roman world, the slavery he commends is not a relation between a master and an inferior whom the master orders and controls. He speaks rather of a *mutual* enslavement, uncoerced, engendered not by fear but by love. This love, Paul knows, creates community; preoccupation with my needs, my rights, my privileges just as surely destroys it. Because the very life-space in which Christian freedom is announced and experienced is a community nourished by love, then, the command to become slaves of one another is counsel as heavy with wisdom as with irony.

After what he has previously said about the Law—it cannot justify (3:11); Christ redeems Christians from its curse (3:13); it is *not* the means by which the inheritance is given (3:18); it cannot bestow life (3:21); it is a guardian from whose authority Christians are now free (3:23-25)—Paul catches his hearers off guard with his affirmation that "the whole Law is fulfilled in one word" (v. 14; NRSV: "is summed up in a single commandment"), namely the love command of Lev 19:18. Is this affirmation inconsistent with his earlier statements about the Law? Most of those earlier statements declare what the Law *does* or cannot do, or they describe the Christian's present situation with respect to the Law's *authority*. In other words, Paul has earlier focused on the Law's *function*. Galatians 5:14, however, says nothing about what the Law does or cannot do; nor does it say anything about the Law's present authority for Christians. At 3:12 Paul had used scripture's term *do* and at 5:3 the verb *keep* (or *observe*) in conjunction with the Law: persons do or keep its commands. At 5:14, however, he says nothing about keeping or doing; his verb is *fulfill*. The root meaning of *plēroun* is to fill, to fill full, to permeate. In the passive voice in verse 14 it may have the more exact sense of being satisfied by or fully expressed by. Now it may well be that Paul would find unobjectionable the affirmation that the whole Law is fulfilled— that is, kept or done—by *persons* who love their neighbors as themselves. Nevertheless, *persons* is not in his sentence. By changing his passive construction to the active, we reveal that the *actual* (as distinct from the grammatical) subject of his sentence is the "one command" to love the neighbor. Thus it is the command to love the neighbor that "fulfills" the Law—permeates the Law and thus fully expresses the Law's purpose. As later writers might put it, the love command is the distilled essence of the Law.

Paul's critics, whether Christian or non-Christian Jews, could, of course, object that the whole Law is by no means "fulfilled" by the love command alone since that command does not incorporate those prescriptions of Torah essential to the distinctive character of God's chosen people. This objection would reveal the different ways that Paul and his critics were using the word *fulfill*: for Paul, the love command fulfills the Law by focusing on its essential purpose; for Paul's critics, God's people fulfill the Law when they abide by its prescriptions, not least those prescriptions that ensure Israel's holiness. Readers of Galatians misunderstand Paul's view if they think that he is dismissing the "ritual" commands of Torah while retaining the "ethical." The distinction is rather between the particular (ethnocentric) and the universal (inclusive) thrusts of Torah. Paul insists only on the universal, the law of love. His critics find that view unacceptably accommodationist.

A final observation about Gal 5:14 is that Paul does *not* say that Christians should obey Torah's command to love the neighbor! Jesus-people do not love because the Law commands it. They love because the Spirit produces its fruit in them (5:22). Because the love command comes from God and because the Spirit is the Spirit of God, it is hardly surprising that the love creative of God's new inclusive people is both commanded by the Law and produced by the Spirit. Nevertheless, for Paul, the dynamics of obeying the Law and being led by the Spirit are fundamentally different. If, living under the Law's regime, I face a situation requiring decision—say, whether to take something that is not mine—I will, finally, do the right and loving thing because the Law says, "You shall not." If I live "in Christ," I will do the right and loving thing because the Spirit is producing its fruit in me. It would appear, then, that in 5:14 Paul is not being inconsistent with his earlier declaration that Christians are no longer under the custody of the Law.

The Works of the Flesh and the Fruit of the Spirit (5:16-26)

The metaphor of wild animals biting and devouring one another (5:15) likely reflects the condition of personal relationships in the Galatian churches. Otherwise the vivid harshness of Paul's language would seem inappropriate and out of place. What was the nature of that conflict, and what was its cause? Theological controversy? Class antagonism? Personality clashes? The Galatians knew. We do not. But the antidote to biting and devouring one another that Paul firmly enjoins is to follow the Spirit's prompting and direction in personal conduct (5:16). Like "run" in 5:7, "walk" (NRSV: "live") is a metaphor of the Christian life that implies movement, purpose, and goal. Uses of this metaphor in Scripture lend the sense of obediently committing oneself to the ways of God (e.g., Deut 5:33; 11:22; 26:17; Ps 81:13), but to Scripture's instruction to walk in God's statutes Paul counterposes walking by the Spirit. Persons who take directions from the Spirit will not "fulfill"—the verb *telein* here (NRSV: "gratify") means to execute or carry out—the desire of the flesh (v. 16). The apostle does not here issue a command (so NRSV). Rather, he affirms a state of affairs. The emphatically negated subjunctive has the force of a future indicative: this *will* not be the case! Why not? Because the flesh and the Spirit, constantly at odds with each other, pull a person in opposite directions. Persons who take their direction (their orientation *and* their marching orders) from the Spirit *can*not carry out the flesh's fundamental desire (despite NRSV, the noun *epithymia* is singular).

More puzzling is the last clause of verse 17: "they oppose (or resist) each other so that you might not do the very things you want [to do]" (AT). The interpretation of this statement commended here rests on one observation and two contentions. The observation is this: Paul does *not* use a verb that means "you cannot, you are not *able*" to do what you will; rather, he uses the verb *do,* and this verb is in the subjunctive mood. The contentions are these: (1) The verb *do* is subjunctive because the conjunction *hina* introduces the clause. This conjunction can signal either purpose ("in order that") or result; in the letters of Paul, however, except when used after certain verbs, *hina* most frequently indicates purpose or goal. We should assume it means "in order that" (purpose) at Gal 5:17 *unless* that meaning prevents the *hina* clause from making sense. (2) The whole of 5:17 constitutes an explanation ("for") in weak parenthesis; it is here to explain why believers who walk by the Spirit can by no means carry out the flesh's desire.

Whether Paul thought of the flesh and the Spirit as powers engaged in cosmic warfare this verse does not reveal. Here he has in view the lives of human beings: "you" is the subject of the verbs in verses 16, 17*d,* and 18. It is with *believers* as the prize that the flesh and the Spirit rise against each other. In the present, neither the flesh nor the Spirit can annihilate the other, but the flesh opposes the Spirit so that believers will not do the bidding of the Spirit, and the Spirit opposes the flesh so that believers will not be agents for the flesh. The flesh and the Spirit oppose each other in order to keep Christians from doing what they might otherwise do if the other adversary were not on the field. The subjunctive moods remind us, though, that Paul is making no assertion about the self, either that the believer's will is paralyzed or that believers find themselves on both sides of the conflict. He is, rather, saying something about the purpose of two antagonists, the flesh and the Spirit: each tries to keep believers from acting in concert with the other. Nevertheless, verse 17 unobtrusively makes the point that the Christian life is not simply a matter of willpower. The deciding self operates in a messy arena—indeed, *as* the messy arena—where contending powers struggle for hegemony. For believers, however, the outcome of this struggle is assured: those persons who allow themselves to be guided by the Spirit will not carry out the desire of the flesh. The Spirit will prevail!

Like verse 16, verse 18 is an assertion rather than an injunction: those who are led by the Spirit are not subject to the Law's authority. One can take orders from only one supreme commander. Accordingly, placing oneself under the Spirit's charge necessarily excludes honoring the Law's authority. Why, though, in a section featuring the conflict between the Spirit and the *flesh* does Paul suddenly reintroduce the *Law?* Why the implied parallel between carrying out the flesh's desire and being subject to the Law's authority (16*b* and 18*b*)? In Paul's binary system, both the Law and the flesh belong in the column set over against the Spirit. Both are agents of an age now obsolete. But the apostle's statement might prompt another realization: for those who are led by the Spirit, the Law is not *necessary.* In Judaism the Law was widely regarded as the divinely-given antidote to the vices of desire. Paul has already declared, though, that the Law cannot give life (3:21). In the present passage, focusing as it does on the *sufficiency* of the Spirit for the Christian life, he implies that the Law is not *needed* as an indicator of unacceptable behaviors or as a moral guide. The works of the flesh (an echo, no doubt, of "works of the Law") are clear and evident even without the Law.

The list of fifteen items that enumerates examples of such "works" (vv. 19-21) would look familiar to any educated person of the hellenistic world, for catalogues of vices and virtues were a standard feature of ethical discourse in Judaism and the philosophical schools as well as in early Christianity. Especially at the beginning and end of his list, Paul names behaviors that any fellow Jew or God-fearer would enthusiastically condemn: sexual immorality, moral impurity, debauchery, idolatry, sorcery, bouts of drunkenness, revelries. Several of these attest his concern about the unrestrained energies of human sexuality. The other eight vices that he includes in his admittedly partial and merely illustrative list ("and things like these," v. 21) all have in common a power to disrupt fellowship and destroy the common life of the Christian community: hatred (enmity, ill will), discord, jealousy, fits of rage, selfish ambitions, dissensions, factions, feelings of envy. It is particularly important for modern readers who associate "the flesh" exclusively with certain physical acts or states (such as sex or drunkenness) to note that two-thirds of the items in this vice list are sins of mind and heart.

Over against the "works of the flesh" that will exclude persons from the kingdom of God, Paul posits the "fruit of the Spirit" (5:22). "Fruit" as a metaphor of the product or consequence of *human* effort is familiar in the Hebrew Bible and Jewish literature. The singular form of the noun is noteworthy. Why not the plural, so as to correspond more exactly to "works"? Love, joy, peace, patience, kindness, goodness, faith (or faithfulness, reliability), gentleness, and self-control (vv. 22-23) are certainly *multiple* traits of character. Perhaps Paul is saying that the Spirit's fruit is not sometimes this, sometimes that; rather, the lives of Spirit-led persons are constantly and consistently marked by all these traits. Or perhaps the single fruit of the Spirit is love and the other eight traits are all love's constituents and manifestations, counterbalancing the eight sins of mind and heart so destructive of community in verses 20-21. In either case, Paul's metaphor suggests that these qualities of character are not the results of human vigilance and determination. They are the unnatural but inevitable produce of God's Spirit energizing, working in and working through, the lives of believers. And, one cannot fail to notice, this particular fruit is precisely what nourishes *community*. Are these qualities of character, unnatural as they are, among the "miracles" that Paul alluded to much earlier (3:5)? Certainly they would be evidence that Christ was being formed in the lives of believers (4:19).

The last quality of character in Paul's "list of virtues," *enkrateia* (self-control or self-mastery), deserves special comment. In Greco-Roman culture, the ethical ideal of moderation (as in Aristotle's "golden mean") required the mastery of powerful desires and dangerous impulses that often seemed deaf to reason's voice. Consequently, much of the ethical discourse of Roman hellenism was preoccupied with that self-mastery essential to moral excellence. Apologetic texts of hellenistic Judaism (Philo, Josephus, 4 Maccabees) presented Judaism as a superior school for self-mastery and the Law of Moses as an unsurpassed means to that goal (Stowers 1994). It is hardly accidental, then, that the last "virtue" in Paul's list is a central ideal of Greek ethics to which hellenistic Jewish authors were eager to lay claim. As the last item in Paul's list, self-control corresponds to the first, love, and these two traits thus "enclose" and frame the others. We might think of self-mastery, the capacity to override one's own natural desires, as the psychological wellspring of that love that loves the neighbor as oneself (5:14) and elevates persons to the status of one another's slaves (5:13). *Self*-control is, nevertheless, an ironic virtue because it is the fruit of the Spirit, *not* a work of the self!

Heard as a forthright declaration, "there is no law against such things" (or "the Law is not against such things") sounds rather banal. If verse 23*b* is instead a deliberate rhetorical understatement, Paul is actually claiming that the character produced by the Spirit fulfills the Law. If here he echoes a popular maxim originating with Aristotle (*Politics* 3.13.1284A), he is asserting that such character in fact makes law unnecessary, for, according to Aristotle, persons who surpass others in virtue themselves constitute a standard. The purpose of the Law is to guard and restrain (3:23-24). But where the Spirit is at work, such guarding and restraining is not needed. That is why "if you are led by the Spirit, you are not subject to the law" (5:18). Just as the Law is not needed to make plain the works of the flesh (5:19), so the Law is not needed to shape the human character that is well-pleasing to God. Where the Spirit is at work, the Law is superfluous. In making the claim that the Law is no longer necessary, of course, Paul ignores those special commands of Torah that serve to distinguish Jews from Gentiles.

In the context of 5:16, 22 on the one side and 5:25 on the other, "those who belong to Christ Jesus" (5:24) are those who are given life by the Spirit and led by the Spirit, those whose character is the fruit of the Spirit. They live in Christ's domain and belong to him by virtue of their life orientation and commitment. For the second time Paul now employs the shocking figure of crucifixion. But here it is not the *egō*, I, which is crucified with Christ (as at 2:19-20); rather, those who belong to Christ have crucified the *flesh* "with its passions and desires." Energized and empowered by the Spirit, persons who live under Christ's lordship put to death the psychical source of the passions and desires and thus attain the self-mastery (v. 23) that allows them to love and serve one another (5:13-14). What Paul says here, then, and what he says at 2:19-20 amount to the same thing.

In 5:21 the apostle issues a warning: those who do such "works of the flesh" will not inherit the kingdom of God. Implicit in verse 24 is a second warning: those persons whose lives do not manifest the "fruit of the Spirit" have *not* crucified the flesh and thus do not belong to Christ.

Because the first clause of verse 25 expresses a condition that is actually the case, the Greek word *ei*, usually translated "if," is here better rendered "since." Paul's earlier description of the children of promise as "born according to the Spirit" (4:29) and his strong implication that only the Spirit can "make alive" (3:21) echo in this directive of verse 25: "Since we have life by the Spirit, by the Spirit let us also walk" (AT). The root meaning of the verb *stoichein* (NRSV: "be guided") is to stand or march in a line and so to walk alongside, correspond to, agree with. Paul thus enjoins the Galatians to take their cue from, to keep in step with, the Spirit. The

Spirit is not only life-giving; it is life-directing as well, leading children of the promise toward the hoped-for goal of righteousness (5:5). Taken together, verses 24 and 25 (crucifying the flesh, following the Spirit's lead) mirror 5:16. Verse 26 then echoes verse 15, and in the wake of that earlier verse one should hear verse 26 as a directive aimed specifically at the situation of the Galatian communities: "Let us not be vainglorious, provoking one another, being jealous of one another." The word here translated "vainglorious" (NRSV: "conceited"), *kenodoxos,* is a composite term, its constituents meaning "empty opinion" (or "empty glory"). Persons who are vainglorious—conceited and boastful—base their view of themselves, and thus of others, on hollow opinion—opinion lacking the substance of fact. The term announces one of the emphases of the following verses.

Nurturing the Community (6:1-6)

The injunction of 5:26 is couched as a negative. Those of 6:1-6 are all positive. Whether these instructions reflect specific problems that were creating disharmony in the Galatian congregations, modern readers have no way of knowing. They could be, rather, "focal instances" illustrating behaviors typical of believers who have become slaves of one another through love (5:13) and who follow the Spirit's lead (5:25). In either case, they all pertain to believers' *responsibility* to ensure the actualizing of genuine *community* among Jesus-people. Paul weaves together directives about conduct directly benefiting *other* members of the community (6:1a, 2, 6) with directives that would ground such conduct in sober *self*-assessment (6:1b, 3, 4, 5).

We should probably think of the person who might be "caught in some trespass" (6:1 AT)—the English word *caught* nicely representing the ambiguity of the Greek verb (be detected or be overtaken or taken by surprise)—as a member of the Jesus-community. But would such a person not be among those who had received the Spirit (3:2) and thus be one of the "spiritual ones" (6:1 NRSV: "who have received the Spirit")? If so, would

and ethical behavior? Or should we assume, rather, that a member
of the Jesus-community caught in some trespass is *not* among the
"spiritual ones"? Should we revisit Gal 3:2-5 and conclude, in
light of 6:1, that Paul is *not* there affirming that every member
of the Galatian congregations had received the Spirit, that there
he refers instead to a particular social or religious *class* of
believers whose experience had been determinative, perhaps, for
persons in their charge such as slaves and client freedmen? In
either of these cases, Paul's if-clause acknowledges that moral
perfection was no more a feature of Jesus-communities in the first
generation than in our own. Even "you spiritual ones" have to be
on their guard, constantly alert, examining themselves so that they
too will not be tempted to sin. Paul implies that if the spiritual ones
reflect on how easy it is to get "caught" in some trespass, their
self-scrutiny can nurture the "spirit of gentleness" that will moti-
vate them to restore an erring brother—restore him to personal
wholeness *and* set him right again with the community. "You
spiritual ones," then, amounts finally to a challenge.

Paul's second imperative acknowledges another sort of difficulty
that could beset the community—not moral failure but those life
experiences that are heavy enough to weigh people down and tire
them out: hardship and deprivation, drudgery and frustration, loss
and disappointment, duty and responsibility. The injunction to
"bear one another's burdens" creates a picture of someone shoul-
dering a load that has become too heavy for another to bear. It is
an image of release and relief. Bearing the burden of another is,
indeed, a metaphor of grace. And bearing *one another's* burdens
highlights the interdependence that makes members of Jesus-
communities instruments of grace to one another. As you do this,
Paul says, you will fulfill the law of Christ. (Other manuscripts have
the aorist imperative rather than the future indicative: "and so fulfill
the law of Christ.") "The law of Christ" appears to be an ironic
Pauline formulation aimed particularly at those who are eager to
be "under the Law" (4:21). What does the apostle mean by this
expression?

Two features of 6:2 would remind attentive hearers of 5:13c-14: the Greek word *one another* (which, aside from 6:2 and 5:13, occurs elsewhere in Galatians only at 5:15, 26 with the "negative" verbs *bite, devour, consume, provoke,* and *envy*) and the verb *fulfill* (*anaplēroun;* cf., at 5:14, the simple *plēroun*). These two points of correspondence suggest that bearing one another's burdens is one way that believers become one another's slaves and, by loving their neighbors as themselves, fulfill the Law. Burden-bearing (6:2), after all, is fitting work for slaves (5:13). With his phrase "the law of Christ," then, Paul provocatively claims and renames that law, the command to love the neighbor, which (according to an early Christian tradition that Paul probably knew) Jesus himself considered central to God's revelation in Torah. The "law of Christ" is indeed that epitome of the Law, the command to love, which Christ exemplified when he "loved me and gave himself for me" (2:20). Christ himself, then, is the foundational paradigm for life in the Jesus-communities of Galatia (Hays 1987).

With the maxim of verse 3 (a maxim that has several approximate parallels in Greek and Roman literature), Paul apparently intends to ground the injunction of 6:2 ("for . . . "), but the precise nature of the connection is not at once clear. Note, however, that in verse 2 he does not say, "Bear the burdens of others." He says, rather, "Bear *one another's* burdens." The emphasis on *mutuality* implies that no one is so self-sufficient as never to have burdens too heavy to bear by oneself. An unrealistic assessment of one's own capacities can make a person aloof to the ideal of mutuality that Paul is insisting upon. If someone thinks he is something when he is nothing—that is, thinks he is something that he isn't—he deludes himself and he is guilty of the "empty opinion," the vainglory, that marks persons who are not in step with the Spirit (5:25-26). Such an attitude thwarts the loving relationships essential to genuine community.

The antidote Paul proposes to the "empty opinion" about oneself that impedes genuine mutuality is clear-eyed self-assessment: "Let each person assay his own work, and then he will have his cause for boasting [or, perhaps, self-confidence] in himself alone and not in the other" (6:4 AT; NRSV renders the verse very differently). Here the apostle presses for a more objective standard of self-evaluation than a comparison of oneself with other people. What one is to assess is one's *work*. Earlier in the letter, this term, in the phrase "works of the Law," bears a negative connotation, but here, in the singular and in the context of 5:13–6:10, it seems to refer to one's contribution to the Jesus-community. Few tests could so effectively counter people's natural tendency to think they are something that they aren't.

In 6:4 Paul articulates a principle: *if* there be reason for boasting, that reason lies in the work itself and not in comparison with others. It may seem surprising that here he acknowledges, at least in principle, legitimate grounds for boasting. With reference to persons' contribution to the community, he wishes to inculcate an appropriate realism, not an inauthentic modesty. Besides, any work that benefits the community is, after all, the fruit of the Spirit and not the result of one's own straining and striving.

Whether the maxim of verse 5 grounds the preceding injunction (*gar* = "for") or stands independently alongside it (*gar* = "indeed, certainly it is the case that"), the word *idios,* "his own, peculiar to himself," picks up the emphasis of "each . . . his own" and "himself alone" in verse 4. Thus "each person will bear his own load" likely means that each member of the community must assume the responsibility of sober self-assessment so necessary for the well-being of the community.

If, in this passage, Paul were issuing instructions affecting individual persons' private and personal commerce with God, the inclusion of 6:6 would hardly be intelligible. But he is not. The framework of his instructions is the Jesus-communities. Verse 6 attests a differentiation between one who teaches the Christian message ("the word") and the one who learns (literally, catechist and catechumen), those persons with greater insight and understanding (perhaps persons who hold recognized "offices" in the congregations) and those who benefit from their instruction and counsel. Verse 6 may circumspectly urge the financial support of the communities' teachers, but "share in all good things" need not be so narrowly heard. Paul's directive implies that the teachers' function is essential to the community. Thus *their* welfare is an appropriate matter for apostolic advice.

The Spirit's Reward (6:7-10)

In verses 7-10 Paul prefaces two final exhortations (vv. 9, 10) with the ultimate rationale and sanction underlying every entreaty and admonishment of the letter: the final destiny that awaits every human being, either personal annihilation or eternal life. Thus he does not hesitate to appeal to his hearers' highest self-interest. His appeal takes the form of a warning. It features a traditional maxim that employs the metaphor of sowing and reaping, a metaphor widespread in biblical and Greco-Roman literature. His introductory admonition, "do not be deceived," is also a traditional device to focus attention and indicate the significance of what follows. In this case, the Galatians' allowing themselves to be deceived would be a serious matter because "God is not scoffed at [NRSV: mocked]" (the verb means to turn up the nose at, thus to treat with contempt, to scorn, mock, disdain, or ridicule). The connection between this declaration and the sowing/reaping proverb Paul leaves unstated. The connecting idea, apparently, is that God is the cosmic guarantor of justice, justice understood as a fitting correspondence between persons' deeds and the personal consequences of those deeds. Were such correspondence lacking, who could take God seriously? Humans could indeed be contemptuous of the deity if there were not an appropriate and inevitable connection between "reaping" and "sowing." *But,* the apostle contends, God is *not* to be scorned; what a person sows, that *is* what he will reap.

Paul elaborates this familiar proverb in the language of early Christian apocalyptic expectation. Like different soils that receive the sown seeds and mysteriously sustain the process by which those seeds become plants bearing grain, the flesh and the Spirit mysteriously transform human decisions into eternal destinies. The metaphor of sowing and reaping suggests decision and the expenditure of energy and resources in anticipation of future benefit. The irony of sowing "(in)to the flesh" is that the flesh has no future! It can produce nothing but the nothingness of death.

Verse 9 makes clear that Paul does not use the metaphor of sowing to depict some one-time act or decision. "So, in doing what is praiseworthy [NRSV: right] let us not grow weary," he writes. The word translated "praiseworthy" names what is beautiful or, in a moral sense, what is noble, honorable, virtuous, or excellent in and of itself. The participle "doing" suggests a manner of life, and the verb implicitly acknowledges that the kind of sowing Paul is talking about is *sustained* effort that can be threatened by fatigue or waning resolve. As incentive for his call to persist, Paul reiterates the promise of eschatological reward: "for at the appropriate time we *shall* reap if we do not become faint" (AT), the "appropriate time" *(kairos)* being the eschatological moment determined by God.

In light of this promised reward, which in the divine scheme of things will surely be forthcoming, Paul issues a final encompassing exhortation: "Therefore, as we have opportune occasion *(kairos),* let us do what is good with regard to everyone—but especially to those who are members of the family of the faith" (6:10 AT). Here *kairos* refers not to the eschatological consummation (as in v. 9) but to any occasion that affords opportunity for doing good. "What is good" (literally, "the good") recalls "goodness" at 5:22, one of the manifestations of the love that is the fruit of the Spirit. The verb here translated "let us do" *(ergazometha)* means to practice, work at, or bring about, and reminds one of "faith working [*energoumenē*] through love" at 5:6 and "his own work [*ergon*]" that each person is to test (6:4). Believers, then, are to exert themselves on behalf of the well-being of all persons as opportune occasions present themselves, but with special concern for persons who belong to the Jesus-community.

In Gal 6:10 Paul calls his fellow believers "members of the household of the faith" (AT). In his culture, the members of a household were an extended family consisting of a *paterfamilias,* his wife, their children, slaves, and freedmen in some sort of continuing client relationship with the master. The extended family of which Paul speaks likewise consists of persons who differed from one another by virtue of their gender, religious-ethnic background, and social class, as well as their levels of spiritual maturity. Their solidarity inheres in their common inheritance as descendants of

Abraham and children of God according to divine promise, through faith (3:26-29). They belong to the "family of the faith," for faith, as it works through love, is their unifying distinctive.

◊ ◊ ◊ ◊

Unlike the detailed ethical teachings of 1 Corinthians, the parenesis of Gal 5–6 seems rather general. Aside from the behaviors and character traits set forth in the vice and virtue lists, only at 5:26–6:6 do the apostle's instructions concerning the life of faith attain a similar degree of specificity. These instructions hardly constitute even a rudimentary ethical program. Possibly prompted by situations in the Galatian congregations, they serve rather to illustrate the kinds of self-oriented and other-oriented behaviors essential to genuine community: gently restore an erring brother, bear one another's life-burdens, examine yourselves and let your sense of your importance depend on what you actually contribute to the welfare of the community, provide for those who nurture you in the faith. Alongside 1 Corinthians or the Sermon on the Mount, such instructions might seem rather pale, even banal; lived out, however, their practical import would be considerable.

One might wonder, though, why such instructions, or vice and virtue lists, or admonitions to become one another's slaves and do good to all are even necessary. If such behaviors are the fruit of the *Spirit*, if the Spirit guides and empowers, why do believers need *Paul's* counsel? Why not leave everything to the Spirit? That Paul is not willing to do that attests the fact that peace and harmony remained goals rather than realities in his Galatian congregations. And that fact, in turn, confronts readers of Galatians with the realization, once again, that Paul's discourse, like the apostle himself, moves in two separate universes. One is the public world of nature and culture, the world of the "flesh," whose characters are emperor and citizens, male and female, slave and free, Jew and Gentile, rich and poor—the world of suffering, desire, and death. The other is the world unseen whose characters (God, Scripture, God's son, the Spirit) and transactions (God's promise to Abraham, Jesus' death "for our sins," God's reckoning faith as righteousness, God's sending the Spirit "into our hearts") lack the actuality of the real for persons outside the Jesus-communities. Believers, of course, inhabit both worlds. If they were citizens only of the world unseen, Paul's exhortations and instructions would be unnecessary. If they lived only in the public world of the "flesh," his exhortations and instructions would be pointless.

Some readers of Galatians may be convinced that Paul's rejection of "legalism" and his insistence on "justification by grace through faith alone" mean that human "works" have no place in God's "plan of salvation," that "works" represent an effort to *achieve* salvation. The themes of divine grace and human faith certainly permeate Galatians. But does not Paul also hold that one's final destiny depends upon *deeds?* Note that his "we will reap" at 6:9 is contingent on not becoming faint or growing weary. Not weary of what? Not weary of doing what is virtuous (v. 9), not faint from doing what is good (v. 10). Is Paul, then, a muddled thinker? Must we admit a contradiction in Galatians between justification by faith and judgment by deeds?

Galatians 5:21 intensifies the question. Persons who practice the works of the flesh, the apostle writes, will not inherit the kingdom of God. He hardly includes this statement merely for the information it bears. He includes it as a *warning.* If, as we must assume, he regards this warning as appropriate, we must conclude that he did not think it impossible for members of the Jesus-communities to practice such works of the flesh. But were these people not justified by God's grace? We recall that Paul does not conceive of the status of being justified apart from the experience of receiving the Spirit. Yet persons who practice the works of the flesh obviously are not led by the Spirit. It would appear, then, that if such people think they are "righteous," in right relationship with God, they are mistaken. Were they *ever* justified, then? To answer affirmatively would seem to be admitting that God's justifying work can be "undone" by humans. Yet Paul's insistence that he refuses to nullify the grace of God (2:21) compels exactly that conclusion, and the language of 5:4—you have "severed yourselves from Christ," you have "fallen out of grace" (AT)—confirms it.

Congruent with these negative images of nullifying or falling out of grace are the positive Pauline metaphors of the Christian life that bespeak movement toward a goal, the necessity of steadiness and staying on course, and the consequences of deviating. Twice Paul speaks of God's *calling* in grace (1:6, 15). It is possible, though, to turn away from the One who calls (1:6). To be *called* by virtue of God's unmerited favor is not to be magically, effortlessly, transported to the point of one's final destiny. Christ's death liberates persons for new life possibilities, but they can give up that costly freedom. Otherwise, Paul would not enjoin the Galatians to *stand firm* and not get caught again in the "yoke of slavery." Persons stand acquitted before their Creator on no other basis than God's unmerited favor, but they can forfeit their justification. Human beings do not become children of God by their own doing. Only a father can adopt a slave as his son. God does not *compel* people to join the family, but if they choose to do so they must act like members of the family. It does not suffice to *feel* like a family member or to answer correctly a list of questions about what being a member of the family entails. What counts is *conducting* oneself as son or daughter.

The appropriate human response to divine grace is what Paul calls *faith*. But faith is not feelings, not even nice feelings about God. Faith is not the mind's assent to certain propositions about Jesus or about one's own sinful state. Faith is the absolute entrustment of the self to God and God alone. Such a handing over entails a life-orientation: the life of a believer takes its direction, like a compass needle, from the beneficent will of God. And because faith is an engaged *commitment* to God that eagerly seeks to express itself in love for God's other human creatures (5:6), it is impossible for Paul to conceive of faith apart from decision and behavior. Faith knows that no human striving can gain God's acceptance; the divine favor is already, always, a given. Nevertheless, faith is not the antithesis of deed. Faith entails deeds necessarily because no human being can be engaged with life without deciding and doing, and faith is a way of engaging life.

It is true, of course, that in Galatians, Paul declares that human beings are justified by faith and *not* by works of the Law, but "works *of the Law*" is a much more restricted category than human deeds generally. The antithesis, then, between faith and works of the Law does not run counter to those metaphors and exhortations throughout Galatians that assume that sustained effort is an essential dimension of faith.

Related to the question of faith and deeds in Paul's understanding of Christian life is the question of the believer as *agent*. Three types of statements in Galatians, when juxtaposed, raise the question. First, Paul's expression "fruit of the Spirit" implies that the dispositions and character traits listed at 5:22-23 are brought forth *not* by believers but by the power of the Spirit working in and through their lives. On the other hand, it is not the Spirit but rather those *persons* who belong to Christ who have "crucified the flesh" (5:24). A person sows either (in)to his own flesh or (in)to the Spirit (6:8); and the maxim "what a person sows, that will he also reap" leads us to infer that, in either case, the sowing is a matter of personal decision. Certainly the imperatives and hortatory subjunctives that Paul issues throughout Galatians imply that the recipients of the letter are capable of deciding to act or to refuse to act upon his admonitions; *they* are the agents responsible for behaviors that nurture human life and community. Finally, two of Paul's directives pose the question of agency with special sharpness: "walk by the Spirit" (5:16 AT) and "let us walk in step with the Spirit" (5:25 AT). The imperative and subjunctive here aim directly at persons as agents, and both presuppose that the believer can make the choice between walking by the Spirit or not walking by the Spirit. So does the clause, "if you are led by the Spirit . . . " (5:18). Believers can choose to be led by the Spirit, or else Paul's directive is pointless. And yet the agent-self that chooses to follow the Spirit's lead, by that very choice surrenders the power and prerogatives of being in charge.

In Paul's view, persons can commit themselves to Christ and choose to put themselves under the Spirit's charge. So long as they walk in step with the Spirit, energized by that divine power, the life they live will be a mysteriously cooperative venture.

The enemy of that venture Paul calls the "flesh," and the flesh further complicates the question of agency. To focus here on but one problem: if those who are "of Christ" have "crucified the flesh," how is it that the flesh is still able to "desire against" the

Spirit (5:17)? Is 5:17 a generic statement about the human condition generally and not about a conflict that Jesus-people experience? To take this view is to hold that the Spirit resists the flesh in everyone. But what is the Spirit doing in the lives of persons who have not received the Spirit by the "hearing of faith" (3:2-5)? On the other hand, if verse 16 speaks of a conflict between flesh and Spirit that is specific to the experience of Jesus-people, how can Paul say that those very people have "crucified the flesh"? Does crucifixion not mean death? In the course of setting forth his claims about the power and sufficiency of the Spirit, Paul raises questions that he does not answer in Galatians.

The admonitions of Gal 5–6 give the impression that Paul is primarily concerned about the inner community life of the Jesus-assemblies (5:15, 26; 6:1, 2, 6, 10*b*). But since God's promise to Abraham embraces *all* peoples (3:8), we can hardly imagine that the apostle to the Gentiles would restrict the beneficiaries of "faith working through love" (5:6) to Christians alone. True, he does not spell out a social ethic in Galatians, but "let us do what is good to all people" (6:10 AT) issues an unmistakable if sketchy blueprint of believers' responsibility in, and to, the world.

As Christians of every generation learn again *how* to let the Spirit lead, they cannot avoid wrestling with the question of the freedom for which Christ has freed them. The task is to appreciate and live out a genuine freedom, diligently refusing to let it degenerate into mere unrestrictedness. At 5:13, in his final affirmation about the vocation of freedom ("you were *called* to freedom"), Paul's wonderful irony holds the key: Christ liberates persons so that they can freely enslave themselves to one another! Freedom provides unencumbered *opportunity* for serving one another, even as slaves, in love. So enslaved, believers are free indeed. From the Pauline point of view, any other "liberation" ushers persons into some other state of bondage.

"Enslave yourselves *to one another*" highlights one of the prominent themes of Paul's Galatian parenesis: *mutuality*. For those who are together "in Christ," genuine mutuality nourishes the oneness of community and disallows attitudes of superiority and inferiority alike. In Christ *all* are recipients of grace. Here, then, the benefactor's patronizing air has no place; nor does the supplicant's embarrassment of need. Where love prevails, both will disappear.

THE POSTSCRIPT (6:11-18)

Paul closes his letter to the Galatian congregations with an epistolary postscript, a conventional feature of the hellenistic letter form. By announcing that he has taken the pen from his amanuensis, he tells his hearers that he is about to conclude. The "large letters" in his own handwriting emphasize and confirm key points of the preceding case that he wants to focus on in this last effort to prevent the Galatians from being swayed by the agitators' appeal. The postscript serves as Paul's official seal upon the whole letter.

◊   ◊   ◊   ◊

The emphases of the postscript provide a final indication of this letter's central purpose and message. Most obvious is Paul's attack on the agitators and his stress on the great divide that separates him from them. They wish to avoid the persecution that the cross of Christ might bring upon them (v. 12); he bears on his body the "marks" of the crucified Jesus (v. 17). They are eager to "boast about your flesh" (v. 13); Paul will boast only in the cross of Christ (v. 14). They are preoccupied with "fleshly" matters important in a world to which he has been "crucified" (vv. 12-14). This effort to distance himself from the agitators corresponds to his earlier accusations (1:7; 3:1; 4:17; 5:7) and his self-presentation as an uncompromising defender of the truth of the gospel (1:13–2:21).

Another obvious emphasis is the cross of Christ (6:12, 14). Numerous times throughout the letter Paul alludes to, or makes affirmations about, the death of Jesus. He reminds the Galatians that the crucified Jesus was at the heart of his initial preaching to them (3:1). The "offense" of the cross stands in sharp contrast to the old mark of belonging to the people of God that the agitators insist upon (5:11). Paul describes the experience of being transformed into a new self as being "crucified with Christ" (2:19). It is inconceivable for him, then, that Christ died to no purpose (2:21). The purpose of that death he states in various images: Christ "gave himself for me" (2:20), "redeemed" those who were under the Law and its curse (3:13; 4:5), and "gave himself for our sins, to rescue us from the present evil age" (1:4 AT). None of these statements, singly or in combination, amounts to a developed "theology of the cross." They do, however, attest Paul's conviction that the crucifixion of Jesus marks the decisive turning point from the old age to the new. Jesus' death is also the necessary pattern of believers' "dying," that loss of self and world that allows for a new configuration of the self, centered now in Christ and sustained by the power of the Spirit. Jesus' death is, as well, the event creative of that new human community that, by emulating his self-giving love, nourishes the new self of every believer.

A third emphasis of the Pauline postscript is the "new creation" of verse 15. The Greek word *ktisis* means "created thing" and can refer to an individual creature or to the whole of the created order—thus, in Gal 6:15, to a *person* or to the *situation* in which persons live out their lives. If we hear verse 15 in conjunction with verse 14, we need not choose between these two. In verse 14 Paul writes that the world had been crucified to him and he to the world. This is no statement of public fact. It is a confession of personal transformation: "the world" has lost its determinative power over Paul; it is no longer "there" for him. And the person who had lived there, *is* no longer. As the preceding phrase "the cross of our *Lord* Jesus Christ" suggests, Paul now answers to a new master. But not Paul alone, for verse 14 is probably not merely an autobiographical assertion. "I" encompasses every person who accepts the challenge to become, like the apostle (4:12), a slave of Christ (1:10). The pronoun is both monitory and inclusive; it encompasses every member of the Jesus-community who, like Paul, has been crucified with Christ.

Galatians 6:15 both echoes and clarifies the affirmation of verse 14. Here, one notes, Paul does *not* say that circumcision amounts to nothing; nor does he set forth uncircumcision as more pleasing to God. He relativizes each state by making *both* irrelevant. He sets both aside in light of a "new creation." These religio-cultural categories simply do not fit what now has come about. What has come about, though, has its own location. The assertion of verse

15 makes sense only within a particular community, that community implicit in the Pauline phrase "in Christ," in the expression "be baptized into Christ" (3:27), and in the figure of Jesus-people as the family of faith (6:10). The formative values and structures of "the world" have disappeared not in the general public arena of the Mediterranean basin but only within a distinctive socio-spiritual "family" where the Spirit is at work transforming Jews and alien Gentiles into brothers and sisters, heirs according to divine promise.

In Jewish and Christian writings, "creation" necessarily implies a creator, and so it does in Gal 6:15: the new creation is the work of *God*, who has called it into being by sending his son into the world and the Spirit of his son into the hearts of all who believe. What is "new" here? A new community of new persons! "New creation" names both new situation and new self, for Paul can conceive of neither apart from the other. The believing "I" is another self, a self configured around a new center, empowered by the energy of the Spirit. But this new self has another "home." The "world," this age and its institutions and customs and values, is its home no longer, not even if those institutions and customs and values are those of a religious tradition as noble as Judaism. Its home is the family of others who look and act like sisters and brothers because thay have all "clothed [themselves] with Christ" (3:27).

Because of its unusual syntax and the phrases "this rule" and "the Israel of God," verse 16 is the most problematic statement in the Galatian postscript and one of the most puzzling in the whole letter. What exactly is the *kanōn,* the standard or measure that Paul would like believers to "walk in line with [NRSV: follow]" (the verb is the same as in 5:25)? The usual answer is that the "rule" is the principle articulated in the preceding verse: religio-cultural distinctions are now irrelevant; all that matters is the "new creation," life in the family of God. When one considers, however, that the "for" with which verse 15 begins might signal that this verse is the grounding for verse 14, another possibility emerges: Paul's "rule" is the principle that the only subject of "boasting" in the Jesus-community will be "the cross of our Lord Jesus Christ." (It would, of course, follow that the circumcision/uncircumcision distinction is now irrelevant.)

"Whoever will walk in line with this rule," the apostle writes, "peace [be] upon them and mercy—and upon the Israel of God" (AT). This syntax seems strange. Why does the prepositional phrase "upon them" intervene between the nouns *peace* and *mercy?* The public reader of the letter in the Galatian assemblies could rely on no meaning-clues from punctuation, because there were none; but a punctuation different from the above might allow a more adequate reading: "peace [be] upon them—and mercy also [be] upon the Israel of God." If one reads verse 16*b* in this way and also notes that the future tense (16*a*) can have a progressive sense, Paul is invoking the blessing of peace upon all who continue to live according to the "rule" that the cross is the sole center of identity and value; upon the "Israel of God" he is invoking God's mercy. He thereby appears to be making a distinction between the "Israel of God" and persons in the Galatian congregations who acknowledge the cross as the source of the new creation and the sole "rule" of Christian life. "The Israel of God" is assuredly the broader grouping. How would the Galatians have heard this phrase? *Not,* likely, as equivalent to that "Judaism" that was Paul's previous home (see "in Judaism" at 1:13). Yet one must be careful not to impose upon Paul's language the later distinction between Judaism and Christianity as separate "religions." Such caution leaves two options. (1) "The Israel of God" echoes "the *ekklēsia* [church] of God" at 1:13 and thus refers to all who have been baptized into Christ (3:27). Upon them Paul invokes the divine mercy, but the encompassing well-being of peace awaits their acknowledging and living solely by the standard of the cross and its "new creation." (2) A second possibility is that the genitive "of God" serves to name the Israel of God's future—not the Judaism of Paul's day but Israel made complete by the inclusion of *all* nations, in accordance with God's promise to Abraham (3:8).

Verse 17 is often read as a stern and solemn demand that Paul's antagonists henceforth leave him in peace. But this verse can be heard as an enthusiastic affirmation. With the expression "the marks of Jesus" the apostle transforms a slave's tattoo or brand into a metaphor of his sufferings on behalf of the gospel (perhaps alluded to at 4:13-14), thus reminding his hearers that he is a slave of Christ

167

(see 1:10). Under the protection of his master and subject to his master's judgment alone, he can be indifferent to the criticism of any and all detractors, including the Galatian agitators and their sympathizers. He is answerable only to Christ. Having made that point, Paul ends the letter with an unconditional blessing upon all its recipients, whom he once again designates fellow members of one family: "May the grace of our Lord Jesus Christ be with your spirit, brothers. Amen." Notable here is the word *spirit* in the singular. In the final line of the letter Paul emphasizes a communal oneness—your [plural] spirit [singular]—which attests the oneness in Christ of all believers.

◊ ◊ ◊ ◊

In the Galatians prescript, Paul affirms that Christ gave himself for our sins so that he might "rescue us out of the present evil age." If one asks *how,* Gal 6:15 provides as good an answer as anything in the letter. "New creation" summarizes what Christ's death makes possible; what, through the Spirit, God is now bringing about; what believers are now becoming; what the inclusive community of God's children *is.* Born of divine grace, sustained in freedom, nurtured by faith, the new creation is taking shape right in the midst of the present evil age, even as believers await the righteousness for which they hope (5:5).

SELECT BIBLIOGRAPHY

WORKS CITED IN THE TEXT
(EXCLUDING COMMENTARIES)

Achtemeier, Paul J. 1990. "*Omne verbum sonat*: The New Testament and the Oral Environment of Late Western Antiquity." *JBL* 109:3-27.

Aune, David E. 1981. Review of *Galatians: A Commentary on Paul's Letter to the Churches in Galatia*, by Hans Dieter Betz. *RelSRev* 7:323-28.

Barclay, John M. G. 1988. *Obeying the Truth: Paul's Ethics in Galatians*. Edinburgh: T & T Clark. Reprint, 1991.

Berger, Peter L. 1967. *The Sacred Canopy: Elements of a Sociological Theory of Religion*. Garden City, NY: Doubleday.

Berger, Peter L., and Thomas Luckmann. 1966. *The Social Construction of Reality: A Treatise in the Sociology of Knowledge*. Garden City, NY: Doubleday.

Betz, Hans Dieter. 1975. "The Literary Composition and Function of Paul's Letter to the Galatians." *NTS* 21:353-79.

Boyarin, Daniel. 1994. *A Radical Jew: Paul and the Politics of Identity*. Berkeley: University of California Press.

Caird, G. B. 1962. "The Chronology of the NT." *IDB* 1:599-607. Nashville: Abingdon.

Charlesworth, James H., ed. 1985. *OTP*. Vol. 2. Garden City, NY: Doubleday.

Dahl, Nils A. 1973. "Paul's Letter to the Galatians: Epistolary Genre, Content, and Structure." Paper presented at the SBL Paul Seminar.

Dunn, James D. G. 1991. "Once More, ΠΙΣΤΙΣ ΧΡΙΣΤΟΥ." In *SBLSP*, edited by Eugene H. Lovering, Jr., 730-44. Atlanta: Scholars Press.

Fredriksen, Paula. 1991. "Judaism, the Circumcision of Gentiles, and Apocalyptic Hope: Another Look at Galatians 1 and 2." *JTS* 42:532-64.

Hall, Robert G. 1987. "The Rhetorical Outline for Galatians: A Reconsideration." *JBL* 106:277-87.

Hansen, G. Walter. 1989. *Abraham in Galatians*. JSNTSup 29. Sheffield: JSOT.

Hays, Richard B. 1983. *The Faith of Jesus Christ: An Investigation of the Narrative Substructure of Galatians 3:1–4:11*. SBLDS 56. Chico, CA: Scholars Press.

_____. 1987. "Christology and Ethics in Galatians: The Law of Christ." *CBQ* 49:268-90.

_____. 1989. *Echoes of Scripture in the Letters of Paul*. New Haven, CT: Yale University Press.

_____. 1991. "ΠΙΣΤΙΣ and Pauline Christology: What Is at Stake?" In *SBLSP*, edited by Eugene H. Lovering, Jr., 714-29. Atlanta: Scholars Press.

Hooker, Morna D. 1989. "ΠΙΣΤΙΣ ΧΡΙΣΤΟΥ." *NTS* 35:321-42.

Hultgren, Arland J. 1980. "The *Pistis Christou* Formulation in Paul." *NovT* 22:248-63.

James, William. 1902. *The Varieties of Religious Experience*. Modern Library. New York: Random House. Reprint, 1929.

Jewett, Robert. 1970–71. "The Agitators and the Galatian Congregation." *NTS* 17:198-212.

_____. 1979. *A Chronology of Paul's Life*. Philadelphia: Fortress.

Johnson, Luke T. 1982. "Romans 3:21-26 and the Faith of Jesus." *CBQ* 44:77-90.

_____. 1986. *The Writings of the New Testament: An Interpretation*. Philadelphia: Fortress.

Kennedy, George A. 1984. *New Testament Interpretation Through Rhetorical Criticism*. Chapel Hill: University of North Carolina Press.

Kinneavy, James L. 1987. *Greek Rhetorical Origins of Christian Faith: An Inquiry*. New York: Oxford University Press.

Knox, John. 1954. *Chapters in a Life of Paul*. London: Adam and Charles Black.

Koester, Helmut. 1982. *Introduction to the New Testament*. 2 vols. Hermeneia FFNT. Philadelphia: Fortress.

Lakoff, George. 1987. *Women, Fire, and Dangerous Things: What Categories Reveal About the Mind*. Chicago: University of Chicago Press.

Lakoff, George, and Mark Johnson. 1980. *Metaphors We Live By*. Chicago: University of Chicago Press.

Lull, David J. 1986. " 'The Law Was Our Pedagogue': A Study in Galatians 3:19-25." *JBL* 105:481-98.

Lyons, George. 1985. *Pauline Autobiography: Toward a New Understanding*. SBLDS 73. Atlanta: Scholars Press.

Mack, Burton. 1990. *Rhetoric and the New Testament*. Minneapolis: Fortress.

McLean, Bradley H. 1991. "Christ as Pharmakos in Pauline Soteriology." In *SBLSP*, edited by Eugene H. Lovering, Jr., 187-206. Atlanta: Scholars Press.

Malina, Bruce J. 1981. *The New Testament World: Insights from Cultural Anthropology*. Atlanta: John Knox.

Martyn, J. Louis. 1985. "A Law-Observant Mission to Gentiles: The Background of Galatians." *SJT* 38:307-24.

_____. 1991. "The Covenants of Hagar and Sarah." In *Faith and History: Essays in Honor of Paul W. Meyer*, edited by John T. Carroll et al., 160-92. Atlanta: Scholars Press.

Meeks, Wayne A. 1974. "The Image of the Androgyne: Some Uses of a Symbol in Earliest Christianity." *HR* 13:165-208.

_____. 1983. *The First Urban Christians: The Social World of the Apostle Paul*. New Haven, CT: Yale University Press.

Mitchell, Stephen. 1992. "Galatia." *ABD* 2:870-72. New York: Doubleday.

Petersen, Norman R. 1985. *Rediscovering Paul: Philemon and the Sociology of Paul's Narrative World*. Philadelphia: Fortress.

Räisänen, Heikki. 1983. *Paul and the Law*. Tübingen: Mohr-Siebeck. Reprint, Philadelphia: Fortress.

Ramsay, W. M. 1899. "Galatia." In *A Dictionary of the Bible*, edited by James Hastings, 2:81-89. Edinburgh: T & T Clark.

Schüssler Fiorenza, Elisabeth. 1983. *In Memory of Her: A Feminist Theological Reconstruction of Christian Origins*. New York: Crossroad.

Shaw, Graham. 1982. *The Cost of Authority: Manipulation and Freedom in the New Testament*. London: SCM. Reprint, Philadelphia: Fortress, 1983.

Smit, Joop. 1989. "The Letter of Paul to the Galatians: A Deliberative Speech." *NTS* 35:1-26.

Stanley, Christopher D. 1990. " 'Under a Curse': A Fresh Reading of Galatians 3.10-14." *NTS* 36:481-511.

Stendahl, Krister. 1963. "The Apostle Paul and the Introspective Conscience of the West." *HTR* 56:199-215. Reprinted in *Paul Among Jews and Gentiles*. Philadelphia: Fortress, 1976.

Stowers, Stanley K. 1994. *A Rereading of Romans: Justice, Jews, and Gentiles*. New Haven, CT: Yale University Press.

Williams, Sam K. 1987a. "Again *Pistis Christou*." *CBQ* 49:431-47.

_____. 1987b. "Justification and the Spirit in Galatians." *JSNT* 29:91-100.

_____. 1988. "*Promise* in Galatians: A Reading of Paul's Reading of Scripture." *JBL* 107:709-20.

_____. 1989. "The Hearing of Faith: ΑΚΟΗ ΠΙΣΤΩΣ in Galatians 3." *NTS* 35:82-93.

Young, Norman H. 1987. "*PAIDAGOGOS*: The Social Setting of a Pauline Metaphor." *NovT* 29:150-76.

COMMENTARIES (BOTH CITED AND NOT CITED)

Betz, Hans Dieter. 1979. *Galatians*. Hermeneia. Philadelphia: Fortress. — The commentary that every subsequent English-speaking commentator refers to as a standard. Especially notable for its rhetorical analysis of Galatians and for its wealth of references to Greek and hellenistic literature. Discussion of Greco-Roman parallels can, however, at times lead readers away from Paul's text rather than deeper into it.

Bruce, F. F. 1982. *The Epistle to the Galatians: A Commentary on the Greek Text*. NIGTC. Grand Rapids, MI: Paternoster and Eerdmans. — A learned clause by clause, phrase by phrase, exegesis of the Greek text by a highly respected evangelical scholar.

Burton, Ernest DeWitt. 1921. *A Critical and Exegetical Commentary on the Epistle to the Galatians*. ICC. Edinburgh: T & T Clark. — One of the great Galatians commentaries, notable for its erudition and critical acumen. An unusual feature is a lengthy appendix consisting of "Detached Notes on Important Terms of Paul's Vocabulary."

Cousar, Charles B. 1982. *Galatians*. Interpretation. Atlanta: John Knox. — Brief and non-technical; does not attempt a verse-by-verse exegesis, but theologically perceptive and highly readable.

Duncan, George S. 1934. *The Epistle of Paul to the Galatians*. MNTC. New York: Harper & Brothers. — Useful non-technical commentary based on the translation of James Moffatt.

Dunn, James D. G. 1993. *The Epistle to the Galatians*. BNTC. Peabody, MA: Hendrickson. — An important commentary by a leading scholar; Dunn evinces an impressive familiarity with contemporary Pauline scholarship and profitably engages the views of others while pursuing his own distinctive interpretation.

Fung, Ronald Y. K. 1988. *The Epistle to the Galatians*. NICNT. Grand Rapids, MI: Eerdmans. — An informed but predictable commentary by a conservative scholar who champions the view of Protestant orthodoxy that in Galatians Paul counters Jewish "legalism" with his doctrine of justification by faith.

Longenecker, Richard N. 1990. *Galatians*. WBC. Dallas: Word. — Thorough and detailed, with useful bibliographies throughout. Particularly helpful are its surveys of scholarly debates regarding disputed points of interpretation.

Matera, Frank J. 1992. *Galatians*. SP. Collegeville, MN: The Liturgical Press/Michael Glazier. — Readable and engaging; one of the best recent commentaries for the general reader. Format for individual sections of the letter features "notes" (technical matters), "interpretation," and useful listings of additional resources for further study.

Meyer, Heinrich August Wilhelm. 1880. *Critical and Exegetical Handbook to the Epistle to the Galatians*. 2nd ed. Translated from the 5th German edition by G. H. Venables; translation revised by William P. Dickson. MeyerC. Edinburgh: T & T Clark. — Masterful exegesis by a discerning student of Paul's language and theology; still a significant scholarly resource.

Schlier, Heinrich. 1965. *Der Brief an die Galater*. 4th ed. MeyerK. Göttingen: Vandenhoeck & Ruprecht. — A significant interpretation of Galatians by a convert to Roman Catholicism; as important among modern German commentaries as Betz is among English-language works.

INDEX